AF225216

Author: Jasmin Haynes

Title: Quick, Fast and in a Hurry

ISBN: 978-1-77371-618-3

Category: SELF-HELP/Mind, Body & Spirit

Publisher: Time4Me

2610 Cheney Street, Atlanta, Georgia 30344

....

Printed in the United States of America

TABLE OF CONTENTS

Thank
You!

ACKNOWLEDGEMENTS

To my beloved husband, Jonathan: Your love has been the light that guided me through the darkest times. You are not only my kindred spirit but also the incredible father of our children. You are the heart of my joy, my strength, and the anchor of our family.

To my miracle son, Phoenix: You are living proof that miracles are real, a beautiful reminder of the extraordinary wonders life has to offer. Your presence fills me with awe every single day.

To my daughter, Poppy: My radiant "ree" of sunshine, your boundless curiosity is like a compass, leading me through life's twists and turns with your ever-bright spirit. You inspire me to keep exploring and learning.

To my mother, JoAnn, my grandmother, Maxine Samantha Russell, and my siblings: Camille, Amber, Lenorra, and Wesley — your unwavering love and support have been my constant strength. Thank you for always having my back.

This book is a tribute to all of you.

Jasmin Haynes

BUILD
GOOD
HABITS

FOREWORD

In today's fast-paced world, the demands on our time are greater than ever. We're constantly pulled in multiple directions—by our careers, families, social obligations, and personal ambitions. The idea of having a moment to breathe, let alone focus on our health, often feels like a luxury most of us can't afford. Yet, it's in the midst of this whirlwind that true transformation becomes possible, and this book, *Quick, Fast, and in a Hurry: 7 Healthy Habits for Busy People,* is a blueprint for achieving that change.

I've known the author for several years now and have witnessed firsthand the incredible journey of transformation that has inspired this work. From the high-stakes world of law enforcement in Los Angeles to the tech industry in Atlanta, and from single life to marriage and motherhood, she has seamlessly transitioned between these worlds, all while maintaining her passion for self-improvement and personal growth. But it didn't come without challenges.

As the pages of this book reveal, she too faced the familiar struggle of balancing success in her career, nurturing a young family, and preserving her health and well-being. What makes this book special is its authenticity. It's not a theoretical guide written from the sidelines; it's a deeply personal and practical handbook born from experience—one that is relatable and actionable for anyone who feels the weight of busy schedules, high expectations, and the nagging worry that personal well-being is slipping away.

Quick, Fast, and in a Hurry offers something rare in the realm of self-help: realistic, bite-sized habits that fit seamlessly into the lives of even the busiest people. There's no long-winded advice about radical overhauls or complex routines that require hours of dedication each day. Instead, you'll find seven habits that are easy to understand, easy to implement, and easy to sustain—habits that make an immediate impact.

I particularly appreciate how each chapter is built around the reality that time is limited. The author provides tools and insights that help readers work *with* their demanding lives, not against them. Whether it's learning to move your body in ways that don't require a gym membership, optimizing nutrition without following an exhaustive meal plan, or carving out moments of reflection in the midst of chaos, the strategies are accessible to everyone, regardless of their schedule or circumstance.

This book is a reminder that taking care of yourself doesn't have to be a grand, all-encompassing task. It's about the small, consistent efforts that accumulate over time. The author's blend of personal stories, practical tips, and a no-nonsense approach to well-being makes this guide not only inspiring but achievable.

So, as you begin this journey, know that you're not alone. Countless others, just like you, are seeking balance in a world that often feels unmanageable. Let *Quick, Fast, and in a Hurry* be your companion as you create space for health, well-being, and joy amidst the busyness of life. It's time to prioritize yourself—quickly, fast, and in a hurry.

Here's to a healthier, happier you.

- Gerry Robert
Speaker and International Bestselling Author of *The Millionaire Mindset, Multiply Your Business* and *Publish a Book and Grow Rich*

INTRODUCTION:
Finding Balance in the Chaos

Life can change in the blink of an eye. One moment you're single, managing a thriving law enforcement career while running a side business in real estate and digital marketing in the bustling city of Los Angeles. Next, you're a wife and mother to two lively toddlers, thriving in a tech industry career in Atlanta, Georgia. Talk about change! It's been a whirlwind journey of transformation, from navigating the fast-paced world of business to embracing the joys and challenges of family life. Amidst this transition, one thing became glaringly clear: I was too busy—too busy for my own health, relationships, and my well-being.

If you're reading this, chances are you're in a similar situation. Perhaps you're juggling a demanding career, personal pursuits, and the complexities of daily life, all while struggling to find time for your health and important relationships. It's a common dilemma in today's fast-moving world, and one that many of us face. The pressure to keep up with everything often leaves little room for self-care, resulting in a constant juggling act with our health and happiness.

Quick, Fast, and in a Hurry was born out of my own journey to reclaim balance and well-being amidst the whirlwind of responsibilities. Like many of you, I found myself overwhelmed, constantly on the go, and struggling to stay healthy while meeting the demands of a busy life. What I discovered, though, is that you don't need hours of free time or major life changes to prioritize your health. You just need the right habits—simple, effective practices that fit into your day, no matter how packed your schedule may be.

This book is designed for people like you—individuals who are striving to stay healthy, nurture relationships, and thrive personally, all while managing a full plate. Whether you're a professional balancing a demanding career, a parent juggling family life, or someone simply trying to squeeze wellness into your hectic routine, the seven habits I'll share are crafted to help you achieve balance without sacrificing other aspects of your life.

Why These Habits Matter

Each of the seven habits is built around a core area of well-being, from mental health and physical fitness to time management and self-care. They are designed to be *practical* and *adaptable*, allowing you to make small but impactful changes that don't require massive amounts of time or energy. These habits are meant to empower you to take charge of your health and happiness, no matter how busy life gets.

We're not aiming for perfection here—this isn't about overhauling your entire life or becoming a wellness expert. Instead, it's about making meaningful progress and discovering how to weave healthier choices into your daily routine. By adopting just a few small but intentional habits, you'll start to see improvements in how you feel, both physically and mentally, and gain more control over your time and energy.

The 7 Healthy Habits

Here's a glimpse of what you'll find in the chapters ahead:

Habit 1: Fuel Up The Mind

This chapter focuses on nurturing your inner strength, purpose, and dreams. It's about reigniting your passions and staying connected to what truly drives you, even when life gets hectic.

Habit 2: Move Your Body

Movement doesn't have to be time-consuming. This habit will show you how to incorporate physical activity into your busy day, helping you stay energized and healthy without needing to set aside hours at the gym.

Habit 3: Watch Your Mouth

Eating well doesn't need to be complicated. This chapter explores how making mindful, smart food choices can fuel your body and mind, even when you're short on time.

Habit 4: Check Your Surroundings

Your environment and relationships greatly impact your well-being. This habit highlights the importance of a strong support system and a positive environment in fostering happiness and health.

Habit 5: Press Pause

In the chaos of a busy life, rest and reflection are vital. Learn the art of pausing, taking breaks, and recharging your mind and body for sustained health.

Habit 6: Work with What You Got

Technology can be a powerful ally in your quest for well-being. This chapter shows you how to use apps and tools to streamline your life, stay organized, and make healthier choices.

Habit 7: Time4YOU

Mastering time management is key to creating space for yourself in your busy schedule. Here, I'll share strategies for making time for what truly matters, ensuring that you prioritize your own needs amidst the chaos.

BONUS Habit: The Business of You

Think of yourself as a business. By applying principles of business strategy to your personal life, you can achieve greater clarity, focus, and control over your well-being.

The Journey Ahead

As you work through these habits, I hope you'll find them to be more than just a list of tasks. These are tools for building a life that feels balanced, healthy, and fulfilling—despite the busy pace of everyday life. Remember, this is a journey, not a race. Progress is more important than perfection. Even if you are only able to pick up 1 of the 7 habits, it can make a world of difference! With small, consistent changes, you can transform your habits and, ultimately, your life.

So, are you ready to reclaim your time, health, and happiness? Let's get it!—one habit at a time.

CHAPTER 1:

Fuel Up the Mind

Before anything, we must first delve into your inner mind and thoughts. Through the hustle and quickness of daily life, cultivating a strong mindset and inner peace is essential to navigating life's challenges with grace and resilience. Therefore, the first healthy habit is preserving and nourishing your inner self. We will explore the vital habit of maintaining mental fortitude and emotional balance. As we explore, I'll offer practical strategies to overcome setbacks and heal from past hurts. We will dive into the transformative power of finding resolution by embracing adversity as a catalyst for growth. Learning how to connect with your inner self can unlock profound insights. Let's get you toward clarity and strength in moments of difficulty!

Throughout this chapter, we'll discuss the benefits of visualization practices, how they help shape our reality, and the importance of staying grounded in the present moment. It's amazing how, by aligning your inner beliefs with your actions and making this a healthy habit, you can reveal solutions to life's most persistent problems and achieve a sense of harmony! It has happened to me, and I want to show you that discovering your authentic self to build inner peace will empower you to nurture a resilient mindset that nourishes lasting well-being.

How Do I Connect with My Inner Self?

Nourishing your inner self is a vital habit that strengthens emotional resilience, mental clarity, and overall well-being. One of the most powerful tools for this connection is meditation. By dedicating just 10 minutes a day to quiet reflection, you can calm your mind and body, releasing tension and revealing inner conflicts. The silence can reveal your discomfort, refocus your intentions, and relax high-strung emotions. Simply focusing on your breath and remaining still allows your inner self to emerge with ease. Meditation helps reignite your intentions and create space for self-awareness, as the simple act of focusing on your breath allows your true self to surface.

Another important aspect of nourishing your inner self is engaging in spiritual practice, regardless of religious affiliation. Whether through prayer, reflection, or a creative hobby that uplifts you, spirituality can help anchor your inner being. Even if you're not religious, committing to an activity that feeds your spirit—such as journaling, walking in nature, or dancing to your favorite jams—can bring a sense of peace and divinity. The key is to consistently engage in activities that resonate with your soul, allowing you to connect more deeply with who you are at your core.

Ultimately, the habit of taking time for yourself or prioritizing self-care—whether through meditation, spiritual practice, or any fulfilling activity—leads to greater alignment with your inner self. In the midst of life's busy demands, it's easy to lose sight of what brings out the best in you. We get so caught up in "being busy" that sometimes we lose touch with what truly matters. Do something that brings you joy and resonates with your inner self daily. By committing to a daily practice, even if it's just for 10 minutes, you create space for jubilation and personal fulfillment. This time for yourself becomes a powerful ritual, replenishing your mindset and reinforcing a foundation of inner peace and strength.

Hear It! Speak It! See It! Feel It!

Hearing, speaking, seeing, and feeling your inner beliefs, dreams, and motivations are powerful daily habits that can transform your life. I truly believe this is one of the most powerful and essential habits! Tune into these core elements, and they become the driving force behind every action. Actively engaging with your inner voice and making it a top priority, reinforces your deepest desires and strengthens your resolve, allowing you to create the life you envision. This practice brings focus, fuels your determination, and aligns your actions with your authentic self. It's this consistent connection with your inner beliefs that empowers you to move mountains and achieve the seemingly impossible.

Hear It!

Hearing your beliefs offers significant benefits because it solidifies them into reality. Just as speaking positive affirmations is empowering, listening to them reinforces their impact. Hearing is a form of believing—it creates an internal echo that affirms your mindset and strengthens your focus. Mantras are a great tool to help you stay aligned with your goals and maintain unwavering confidence. Consistently listening to your beliefs, they become a more present and tangible part of your life, helping you stay centered on what truly matters.

This practice also speaks to the subconscious mind, allowing your brain to absorb and retain positive messages without conscious effort. Just as you might remember the lyrics to a song without trying, repeated exposure to affirming statements allows them to stick in your subconscious. Studies show that sound repetition through theta and beta waves enhances brain productivity and efficiency, meaning that listening to positive affirmations helps your mind internalize and act on them. Your subconscious begins to align with your beliefs, giving you the mental green light to move forward with confidence.

Understand that hearing your beliefs acts as a powerful counter to negative thoughts and fears. When faced with a difficult situation, having those affirmations ingrained in your mind allows them to surface when you need them most. This not only helps you manage challenges but actively brings real benefits to your life, guiding you toward resilience and success. Hey, Now that's POWERFUL!

Speak It!

Speaking your beliefs into existence is an interesting habit. Each word spoken can shape your reality. The way we speak to ourselves influences our perception of the world and, ultimately, how we act. A part of your brain, called the Reticular Activating System (RAS), filters out unnecessary information and brings to your attention what matters most. Verbally reinforcing your goals and desires, programs your brain to focus on opportunities that bring those beliefs to life. Speaking your intentions clarifies them and makes them feel more achievable.

There's something uniquely powerful about voicing affirmations that brings them into reality. It's like taking a seed—an idea or thought—and helping it sprout into existence. When you speak your beliefs out loud, it's as if you're giving them the energy to break through the surface, becoming tangible and real for the world to witness. Whether you're affirming your goals while applying makeup or shaving, those small moments of self-affirmation can anchor your beliefs in your daily life. With each spoken word, you're reminding yourself that "I'm here, I am," planting seeds of confidence and determination that grow into real outcomes.

Words are incredibly powerful. As the old adage states, "sticks and stones may break my bones, but words will never hurt me," I believe that this is a crock of shit! Contrary to the old saying, words have the ability to hurt, heal, or elevate us. How we speak to ourselves can have a profound effect on our mindset and self-worth. Just as negative words can tear down, positive affirmations can build up, propelling you toward a greater version of yourself. When speaking affirmations, you're tapping into the transformative power of language, using it to shape your reality and rise above limitations. Words can either be weapons or tools for growth, so choosing them wisely ensures that your beliefs work in your favor, empowering you to manifest your best self!

See It!

Visualization is HUGE for bringing your dreams into existence. It sets things in motion by making them feel real in your mind. Our brains often struggle to distinguish between reality and imagination. It blurs the lines between what we've accomplished and what we've only envisioned. Vividly picturing your goals activates the same neural networks that would be activated by actually achieving them! This tricks the mind into believing that success has already happened, which naturally boosts confidence, motivation, and performance. When using the habit of visualizing success—whether in a presentation, taking on a new venture, or just striving for peace in your life—you're essentially rehearsing for it.

Think I'm making things up? Let's talk about research regarding the "eye/brain duo." The Eye/Brain Duo refers to the powerful connection between what we see and how our brain processes and interprets that information, shaping our perception of reality. When we see something, our brain immediately works to fill in any gaps, creating meaning and stories based on past experiences, beliefs, and assumptions. This process is so seamless that we often believe we're seeing objective truth, even though much of what we perceive is constructed by our brain. This ability to fill in blind spots helps us make sense of the world but can also solidify our perceptions. When we see ourselves succeeding, our brain works hard to fill in the details, making that vision feel more attainable.

In achieving a goal, the eye/brain duo plays a crucial role in helping us "see" the future we want to create. Visualization taps into this connection by allowing us to craft a mental image of success. Because the brain struggles to distinguish between imagined and real experiences, these visualizations feel real. This process strengthens our belief in our ability to achieve our goals, aligning our mindset and actions with the vision we've created. By giving ourselves an incredible story to follow, we leverage the power of the eye/brain duo to turn our dreams into reality, guiding us toward the actions and opportunities that bring us closer to our goals.

Overcome Setbacks

Sometimes, an extra push may be required to overcome tribulations. Finding resolution to setbacks and hurt requires inner strength and a resilient mindset. One of the first steps is to face adversity head-on. Often, we tend to avoid or run away from painful situations, imagining them as insurmountable challenges. It can feel like walking into a cage with a lion, ready to pounce at any moment. But when we confront our fears, we often discover that what seemed terrifying is much smaller and more manageable than we thought. The "lion" may just be a "mouse," offering us an opportunity for growth, learning, and self-discovery. Facing your fears and setbacks instead of hiding from them, builds confidence in your ability to handle any challenge that comes your way. The mindset you cultivate here is key—believing in your strength to overcome obstacles is what transforms adversity into growth.

With setbacks, it's also important to allow yourself to fully experience your emotions. Many of us grew up being told to suppress our feelings, whether it was crying, anger, or even too much laughter. While these limitations were often imposed with good intentions, the result is that, as adults, we sometimes continue to hold back emotions, believing that being stoic is the only way to appear strong. But true strength comes from acknowledging and expressing your emotions. Whether you cry, scream, or laugh until your stomach hurts, releasing emotions helps reduce stress and prevents emotional buildup, which can manifest as physical health problems. Giving yourself permission to feel can make you emotionally healthier and more resilient, allowing you to heal from setbacks faster.

Sometimes, the weight of setbacks and hurt can be too much to bear alone, and that's okay. Seeking counseling or therapy is a valuable tool for working through emotional pain, even when you aren't experiencing extreme trauma. Therapy provides a safe, confidential space to unpack your thoughts and feelings without judgment. Many workplaces offer free counseling services, which should not be overlooked. A professional therapist can help guide you through the healing process, offering insights and strategies to build your inner strength and keep your mindset on track. This is SO ESSENTIAL! Mental health consistency aids self-care and mental resilience, ensuring you stay emotionally grounded and empowered to handle life's roller coaster.

Inner Beliefs Reveal Answers

Inner beliefs reveal answers in profound ways, often through our reactions, emotions, and focused thoughts. One of the clearest ways your inner beliefs manifest is through your reactions to different situations. When faced with a challenge or decision, paying attention to how you instinctively respond can offer deep insights. Ask yourself: Was my reaction positive or negative? Did it leave me feeling anxious or at peace? When reflecting on these questions, you tap into your inner beliefs, which are guiding your feelings and choices. TRUST YOUR GUT! Your gut reaction is often a powerful indicator of what you truly believe and can help point you toward the right course of action.

Emotions also provide a window into your inner beliefs, especially difficult emotions like fear. While fear is uncomfortable, it's an important signal that something unresolved is lying beneath the surface. When fear arises, it's an opportunity to pause and ask, "Where is this coming from?" This line of questioning helps uncover limiting beliefs or past wounds that need healing. Although it may feel daunting, working through these emotions can bring clarity and lead you to the answers you seek. Fear, when examined, can also reveal areas of growth and transformation that guide you toward resolution.

Focused thought is another way to access the wisdom of your inner beliefs. When a problem or question lingers in your mind, dedicating time to quiet reflection or meditation can help bring clarity. Whether through quiet contemplation or active problem-solving, inner beliefs often rise to the surface when given the space and attention to do so. In moments of silence, your mind has the space to untangle the thoughts and beliefs that underlie the issue at hand. When focusing deeply and allowing your thoughts to flow, you can trace the origins of your beliefs and discover answers.

Stay Present

Being content with the present and your current life is essential because it frees you from the hold of the past and helps you embrace the present moment fully. Acknowledging the good that you already have in your life is the foundation for all abundance. As author Eckhart Tolle suggests, whenever you interact with people, don't be there primarily as a function or a role, but as the field of conscious presence. You can only lose something that you have, but you cannot lose something that you are.

When you focus on the present, you release the emotional baggage and barriers tied to past experiences. The past, after all, is behind us, and holding onto it can prevent us from moving forward. It's like driving a car while constantly looking in the rearview mirror—you're bound to crash. The best drivers are the ones focused on the road ahead, adjusting to the present conditions and making decisions based on what's happening now. By being present, you empower yourself to let go of what was and embrace what is, which allows for personal growth and healing.

Being satisfied with the present is important because the future is never guaranteed. We often spend time planning and hoping for a perfect future, but life is unpredictable, and we can't always control what's ahead or behind. While it's good to plan, predictions are not promises. Staying in the present allows you to enjoy what is happening now without constantly worrying about what might or might not come. Since we never know when life may take a turn or when our time will run out, appreciating and being grateful for today brings peace and fulfillment. Living in the moment, cultivates a mindset of gratitude and flexibility, ready to face whatever life brings while finding joy in the here and now.

Build Confidence

The subject of confidence, I would love to write a whole book on! Confidence is a skill that requires continuous development, much like preparing to conquer a mountain. At its core, confidence is the belief in your own abilities and qualities, and it plays a significant role in both success and personal fulfillment. When we lack confidence, we can feel constrained, overwhelmed, or hesitant to take action, even when we have the necessary tools or ideas. Research reveals that self-confidence is considered one of the most influential motivators and regulators of behavior in people's everyday lives. A growing body of evidence suggests that one's perception of ability or self-confidence is the central mediating construct of achievement strivings.

Cultivating inner strength and self-assurance is key to overcoming destructive feelings. Confidence enables you to approach tasks with a sense of capability and determination, allowing you to move through challenges with greater ease. It's essential to focus on building that "confidence muscle" over time, just as you would in any other area of self-improvement.

One of the most effective ways to build confidence is by taking action and accomplishing goals. Each small victory adds to your belief in your ability to succeed, creating a positive feedback loop that encourages you to tackle more ambitious tasks. Tracking your progress is another powerful way to maintain momentum—when you see how far you've come, it reinforces your sense of competence and fuels further growth.

Confidence is also closely linked to integrity and character; when you live in alignment with your values, you naturally feel more self-assured because you trust in yourself. When happy with the present, taking a stance, and thinking like a marathoner—pacing yourself and persevering—you gradually build resilience, which further solidifies your confidence.

The benefits of confidence are profound. Being self-assured empowers you to take risks, embrace new opportunities, and persist in the face of setbacks. Confidence gives you the courage to step outside of your comfort zone and achieve things you once thought impossible. It moves mountains by shifting your mindset from "I can't" to "I will." With confidence, fear becomes less of an obstacle, and challenges become opportunities for growth. This inner strength creates a foundation for lasting success, propelling you to keep striving, even when faced with adversity. The unstoppable YOU!

Quick Tips for Building Confidence

1. **Take Action** – Confidence grows with every achievement.

2. **Track Your Wins** – Keep a record of your progress.

3. **Be True to Yourself** – Integrity strengthens your confidence.

4. **Embrace Positivity** – Find joy in the process.

5. **Stand Your Ground** – Assert your beliefs and values.

6. **Pace Yourself** – Approach challenges with endurance, like a marathon runner.

7. **Fear Less, Do More** – Push past fear to reach your goals.

Elevate Dedication and Determination

Confidence is the ignition to steadfast dedication and determination. Dedication and determination are powerful forces that can help you move mountains by turning intention into action. When you are fully committed to something, you invest your entire energy, focus, and effort into achieving it. This level of commitment sharpens your mindset and strengthens your resolve, making your mind a powerful tool to overcome any obstacles. Dedication means you are unwavering in your pursuit, not easily swayed by doubt or outside influences. No one can convince you to quit or abandon your goals because your dedication acts like a shield, protecting your vision from distractions and setbacks. It transforms mere desires into concrete actions, allowing you to push through challenges with greater ease and confidence.

Determination adds fuel to your commitment, turning it into an unstoppable force! Think about a time when you were absolutely determined to achieve something, like satisfying an intense hunger or pursuing a deeply personal goal. When you're determined, nothing can stand in your way—you'll find solutions, take risks, and persevere, no matter the difficulty. Determination allows you to power through obstacles because you're driven by a need or a desire so strong that quitting simply isn't an option. It's this unrelenting spirit that helps you knock out adversity.

Dedication and determination provide crucial support to your inner self. Committing fully to your personal growth and well-being is one of the most loving and empowering things you can do. Often, we dedicate ourselves to others, external goals, or societal expectations, forgetting the importance of dedicating time and energy to ourselves. When you set goals and dedicate yourself to your own well-being, you reinforce your inner strength and resilience. This self-commitment helps you prioritize what truly matters—your growth, happiness, and fulfillment. Ultimately, by being dedicated and determined for your own sake, you build a foundation of self-love and inner confidence that empowers you to overcome any obstacle and reach your highest potential.

Your Reasons. Your Why.

Why are we doing this? Having a clear "why" is crucial because it anchors you in purpose, providing motivation and direction, especially during tough times. Your "why" is the deep reason behind your actions, and asking yourself, "Why am I doing this?" helps solidify your commitment to any goal. It's what pushes you forward when challenges arise, serving as both a motivator and a protective force. Think of it as your umbrella when life's storms hit and your blanket when adversity chills your spirit. Without a defined reason for your efforts, you may lose focus or energy. But when you know your "why," it becomes easier to keep going, no matter how difficult the journey becomes. Before starting any project or forming a habit, it's essential to define your purpose clearly so that you can navigate the tough moments with confidence and resilience.

Finding your "why" is also about discovering the purpose behind your actions. When you seek clarity on why you're doing something, it sharpens your focus and helps you commit fully to the path ahead. Purpose-driven actions lead to more meaningful results because they come from a place of intentionality.

To uncover your purpose, you need to ask yourself important questions: What do you want? What does success look like to you? Once you define what success means personally, create a vivid mental image of yourself achieving it. Additionally, aligning your goals with your personal values adds depth and commitment to your journey. Purpose isn't just about big life decisions; it's about bringing intentionality to every action, making each step more focused and meaningful.

Finally, it's important to recognize that your "why" should balance both your responsibilities to others and to yourself. While it's admirable to do things for your family, team, or those depending on you, you can't give 100% to others if you're not fully caring for yourself. Your motivation should include taking care of your own well-being because if you're depleted, it becomes impossible to show up for others in a meaningful way. Please let this echo: Whether you're driven by the desire to support loved ones or to achieve personal fulfillment, your "why" must keep you grounded in your own needs too.

Final Thought

Fueling your mind is the foundation of true well-being. Embracing the practice of self-reflection, nurturing your inner peace, and harnessing the power of visualization, you open the door to clarity, strength, and resilience. There are profound health benefits as well. Don't believe me? Research from the NIH highlights the strong connection between human mental health and the reduction of stress, anxiety, and hypertension, along with increased immunity. Life's challenges are inevitable, but with the right mindset, you can transform adversity into opportunity for growth. Through this chapter, you've gained practical tools to heal, overcome setbacks, and align your beliefs with your actions. As you continue to strengthen your mental and emotional fortitude, you'll uncover new insights and solutions to life's struggles, creating a life of balance and harmony. By nourishing your inner self, you pave the way for lasting transformation and a more empowered, fulfilling journey ahead.

CHAPTER 2
Move Your Body

Disclaimer

Before we dive into exercise or movement, I want to make a statement about body image—specifically, the importance of maintaining a positive body image. How we feel about our bodies has a direct impact on how we feel internally about ourselves. There are definitely external factors out there affecting how we should accept our natural forms, both intentionally and inadvertently. It's a battle. However, just remember to keep up the good fight. As Elizabeth Halsted, Ph.D., suggests, Understand the connection between a positive body image and the three things that can help you sustain that "goddess body mentality": self-esteem, emotional stability, and a positive attitude. Remember, it is our image in our minds, and we are in charge of creating it.

Find Time for Exercise

During the chaos of our always-on, fast-moving world, where every minute seems to be accounted for, finding time for exercise is plain old hard! With calendars fuller than a holiday buffet and to-do lists breeding like rabbits, staying active isn't just important—it's your secret weapon against turning into a human pretzel from stress. Hey, I get it! This chapter explores the many ways jam-packed lives can carve out time for exercise, delving into various forms of physical activity tailored specifically for those on the go. From the serene practice of yoga to heart-pumping cardio sessions and muscle-strengthening routines, there is help. Let's uncover the secrets to integrating exercise seamlessly into even the busiest of lifestyles.

Yoga Magic

Yoga is not just a form of exercise; it's a holistic practice that encompasses physical postures, breath control, and meditation. It has been practiced for thousands of years, originating in ancient India. Its effectiveness in promoting holistic well-being has been recognized by modern science, with numerous studies documenting its positive effects on mental and physical health. Yoga works by integrating movement, breath, and mindfulness to create a state of harmony and balance within the body and mind. Its benefits extend beyond the physical realm, touching the mind, body, and spirit.

Central to yoga is the practice of pranayama, or breath control. Conscious breathing techniques help regulate the flow of energy (prana) in the body, promoting relaxation, stress reduction, and increased vitality. Deep, mindful breathing oxygenates the blood, calms the nervous system, and clears the mind, fostering a sense of inner peace and tranquility.

Yoga offers powerful tools for calming the mind and managing stress. Through focused attention on breath and movement, practitioners cultivate mindfulness, learning to observe and detach from their thoughts and emotions. This heightened awareness fosters mental clarity, emotional resilience, and the ability to respond to life's challenges with equanimity.

At its core, yoga is a physical practice involving a series of postures (asanas) designed to stretch, strengthen, and balance the body. These postures target different muscle groups, promoting flexibility, endurance, and muscular strength. Through regular practice, individuals experience improved posture, reduced tension in muscles and joints, and enhanced overall physical vitality.

One of the beauties of yoga is its accessibility to people of all fitness levels and body types. With its gentle, low-impact movements, yoga can improve flexibility, strength, and balance without putting undue stress on the joints. This makes it an ideal form of exercise for individuals recovering from injuries or dealing with chronic conditions.

Yoga is basically the Swiss Army knife of exercise—strength training, flexibility, and mindfulness all rolled into one stretchy, zen-filled package. Who has time to juggle multiple workouts when you can strike a pose and get it all done in 15-30 minutes? No gym membership? No problem! You can downward dog in your living room, warrior pose in your office, or even sneak in a tree pose while waiting for your coffee to brew. So, if your schedule is as packed as a jar of pickles, yoga might just be the life hack you need—no commute, no hassle, just you, your mat, and possibly a very confused pet watching you!

The efficacy of yoga in promoting holistic well-being is supported by a growing body of scientific research. Studies have documented its positive effects on various aspects of health, including stress reduction, pain management, cardiovascular health, and mental well-being. Yoga's ability to modulate the body's stress response, improve autonomic function, and enhance neuroplasticity underscores its potential as a therapeutic tool for promoting overall health and vitality.

In essence, yoga works miracles by harmonizing the body, mind, and spirit, fostering a state of balance, vitality, and inner peace for as little as 10 minutes a day. Its transformative effects extend far beyond the physical realm, touching the depths of our being and awakening us to the inherent wholeness and interconnectedness of all life.

Cardio Helps: HIIT It and Quit It

Cardiovascular exercise, often referred to simply as cardio, is essential for maintaining heart health and overall fitness. Whether it's brisk walking, running, cycling, or dancing, getting your heart rate up has numerous benefits.

At its core, cardio exercise strengthens the heart muscle, enhancing its ability to pump blood efficiently throughout the body. This improved circulation not only lowers blood pressure but also reduces the risk of cardiovascular diseases such as heart disease and stroke. Optimizing the delivery of oxygen and nutrients to tissues and organs, cardio fosters vitality and longevity.

Regular cardio workouts positively influence cholesterol levels, promoting a healthy balance of HDL (good) and LDL (bad) cholesterol. This, in turn, helps to prevent the buildup of plaque in the arteries, reducing the risk of atherosclerosis and related complications. Moreover, cardio boosts metabolism, facilitating weight management and enhancing overall metabolic health.

Cardiovascular exercise not only strengthens the heart but also improves lung function. By increasing respiratory rate and oxygen intake, cardio enhances lung capacity and efficiency, boosting endurance and stamina. This improved respiratory function is particularly beneficial for individuals with respiratory conditions such as asthma, as it enhances their ability to engage in physical activity without discomfort.

Engaging in regular cardio exercise can significantly improve sleep quality and duration. By promoting relaxation and reducing stress, cardio helps regulate sleep patterns, making it easier to fall asleep and stay asleep throughout the night. Additionally, the energy-boosting effects of cardio can enhance daytime alertness and productivity, leading to a greater sense of vitality and well-being.

The benefits of cardio extend beyond the physical realm, profoundly impacting mental health. Engaging in cardiovascular exercise triggers the release of endorphins, neurotransmitters that act as natural mood elevators, leading to feelings of euphoria and well-being. Regular cardio workouts have been shown to alleviate symptoms of depression, anxiety, and stress, promoting mental clarity and emotional resilience.

For us busy bees, squeezing in cardio can feel like trying to fit a treadmill into a closet—challenging, to say the least. But good news! You don't need to spend hours huffing and puffing. High-Intensity Interval Training (HIIT) is basically the espresso shot of workouts—quick, intense, and guaranteed to wake you up. Just 7-20 minutes of alternating between all-out effort and catching your breath can deliver serious benefits. So, if you're short on time but still want to break a sweat, HIIT lets you work hard, rest a little, and get back to your busy day before your coffee even gets cold!

Cardio exercise is a cornerstone of a healthy lifestyle, offering a myriad of benefits for both body and mind. From strengthening the heart and improving circulation to boosting mood and enhancing sleep quality, cardio plays a vital role in optimizing overall health and vitality. So, lace up your sneakers, hit the pavement, and let your heart lead you to a healthier, happier life.

Strength Training: Lift Heavy, Stay Ready

Strength training, also known as resistance training, is often associated with bodybuilders and athletes. However, its benefits extend far beyond simply building muscle mass.

Aging is often accompanied by a gradual loss of muscle mass and strength, a condition known as sarcopenia. Strength training serves as a powerful countermeasure, stimulating muscle growth and preserving muscle tissue. This not only maintains physical strength but also promotes functional fitness, enabling individuals to perform everyday tasks with ease and independence. From carrying groceries to climbing stairs, a strong musculoskeletal system is essential for maintaining mobility and quality of life as we age.

Beyond its effects on muscles, strength training plays a crucial role in maintaining bone density and strength. Subjecting bones to resistance, strength training stimulates bone remodeling, leading to increased bone mineral density and reduced risk of osteoporosis and fractures. This is especially significant for postmenopausal women and older adults, who are particularly vulnerable to age-related bone loss.

Strong muscles are also essential for maintaining proper posture, balance, and coordination. Strength training exercises target key muscle groups involved in posture and stability, helping to correct imbalances and improve alignment. This reduces the risk of falls and injuries, particularly in older adults, while enhancing overall body awareness and control.

It even revs up the metabolism and promotes fat loss. Unlike traditional cardio exercises, which primarily burn calories during the activity, strength training elevates the metabolic rate even at rest, leading to increased calorie expenditure throughout the day. This makes it an effective tool for weight management and body composition optimization, helping to sculpt a leaner, more defined physique.

Interestingly, strength training isn't just about physical transformation; it's also about mental resilience and confidence. Achieving personal bests, overcoming physical challenges, and witnessing tangible progress in strength and muscle tone can boost self-esteem and mental well-being. The sense of empowerment and accomplishment gained from mastering new exercises and reaching fitness goals transcends the gym, positively impacting various aspects of life.

Busy folks often think strength training requires a secret stash of extra hours—spoiler alert: it doesn't! You don't need to dedicate your life to the gym or bench-press your schedule into submission. In just 20-30 minutes, you can squeeze in a solid workout and still have time to binge the trending streaming show (or do it while watching). From you're rocking bodyweight moves, wrestling with resistance bands, or making friends with dumbbells, there's always a way to get stronger without turning your calendar into a battlefield. So, no excuses—Heyyy, flexibility isn't just for yoga!

So, if you're young or young at heart, incorporating strength training into your routine can unlock a world of physical and mental benefits that enrich your life in countless ways.

New Thoughts on Exercise

Exercise trends are constantly evolving so I wanted to give insights to that. The advances in fitness science and changing societal attitudes toward health and wellness just in the past 10 years has been phenomenal!

I remember traditional exercise approaches often focused on long, steady-state cardio sessions or isolated strength training exercises. It's different now. There has been a shift toward more efficient and dynamic workouts, such as HIIT and functional training, that deliver maximum results in less time and we are all here to save time, right!

HIIT (High-Intensity Interval Training) has gained popularity for its ability to torch calories, boost metabolism, and improve cardiovascular fitness in a fraction of the time of traditional workouts. You alternate between periods of high-intensity exercise and short rest intervals, HIIT workouts challenge both the cardiovascular and muscular systems, leading to greater overall fitness gains. Innovative, fun fitness trends keep popping up too! Goat yoga captured the public's imagination. Combining the ancient practice of yoga with the playful presence of goats, this trend offers a unique and lighthearted approach to exercise. There's also rucking, reverse running, and biohacking that are trending movement setters!

So, whether you're into intense workouts like HIIT or something more quirky like goat yoga, there's something out there for everyone. The key is finding what makes you feel good and keeps you healthy.

Body Image Redefined

In the past, body image was often exalted for being slender and lean with little body fat. Remember Jane Fonda workouts! Especially for women, we were held to a standard that was unachievable and an unrealistic expectation. I have yet to see a person who truly looks like Barbie (without surgical intervention). With the inclusion of more diverse voices in business and culture, those high standards have changed. Science has also conducted helpful studies on the reality of how our bodies are composed. Even Barbie has been reconfigured to reflect a more realistic body type. Did you see the movie?

I absolutely love the yoga instructor Jessamyn Stanley, who has created the "Fat Femme" campaign. This woman has not only changed how we look at yoga culture but has reshaped what fit and healthy can mean and look like. I encourage you to check out her Instagram.

The focus is now on how we perceive ourselves and how our perceptions affect our body image. One of the biggest influences is the media and its projection of how we should see ourselves, defining how we should look. I encourage you to turn it off when you can! However, there is a growing counter-movement, with many institutions working to eradicate those pressures. Initiatives such as the Health at Every Size (HAES) Movement, the Body Positive movement, and even companies like Dove have committed themselves to promoting positive body image. Have you seen the commercials?

Think Inner and Outer Health!

"For beautiful eyes, look for the good in others; for beautiful lips, speak only words of kindness; and for poise, walk with the knowledge that you are never alone."

— Audrey Hepburn

As we continue to dive into the habit of moving, don't forget about the inner "muscles" that need strengthening as well. Fostering inner beauty, your gorgeousness and self-worth requires as much "workout" as your physical body and biceps. This inner work can give you that extra boost when pushing through a tough run or challenging treadmill session.

Sweat Happens, Enjoy It

Enjoying exercise is key. It keeps you from going off track—literally and figuratively. Shifting your mindset from "Ugh, I have to work out" to "Sweet, I get to work out!" is like upgrading from a flip phone to a smartphone—it just makes everything smoother. So why do our New Year's resolutions disappear faster than free snacks in the office? It's all about emotions! Studies show that when we actually enjoy exercise (yes, it's possible), we're way more likely to stick with it. So, find a workout that makes you smile—whether it's dancing, lifting, or chasing your runaway dog—and you'll stay on track without even realizing it!

It gets you excited about staying healthy! Shouldn't we focus less on the effort of getting up early or the exhaustion from pumping iron, and more on the benefits of exercise? Exercise has a multitude of benefits that help keep us healthy, especially for those of us with busy lives. Exercise can make you a more energized and focused person, boosting confidence and mood, reducing stress, and improving cognitive function. It's better for your business and your health.

Enjoying exercise isn't just good for your health—it's a magnet for like-minded people. When you actually have fun while working out, you radiate the kind of energy that makes others want to join in (or at least not run away when you suggest a group jog). Dancing like nobody's watching, blasting your favorite pump-up playlist, or simply shifting your mindset, staying active can turn into a social superpower. Plus, that gym buddy could turn into a business partner, a new best friend, or even your next Boo Thang—how romantic is bonding over sore muscles and post-workout smoothies!

Ways to Move While Traveling

Continuing your exercise routine while traveling is essential for maintaining your health and energy. Travel shouldn't derail your fitness goals, whether you're visiting Aunt Sally or meeting a client in another state. You can still move!

At the airport: During long layovers, get creative with staying active. The act of getting to the airport and carrying luggage, briskly walking or running to your gate, already helps burn calories. So take another brisk walk or jog through the terminal while waiting. Do squats, lunges, planks, or other bodyweight exercises. Stretch, or if you can find an empty room or vacant space, practice some yoga. Airports like Dallas-Fort Worth even offer gyms and workout spaces. And yes, I've personally turned LAX into my own marathon training ground—nothing says peak athleticism like jogging through terminals with a carry-on in one hand and a boarding pass in the other. (*Pro tip: dodging rogue luggage carts and oblivious travelers isn't just survival—it's elite-level agility training. Bonus points if you hurdle over a suitcase!*)

Suggestions: Staying active during your actual flight.

- **Seated leg lifts:** Extend one leg at a time and hold it parallel to the ground for a few seconds, then lower it slowly.

- **Ankle circles:** Rotate your ankles in both directions to keep blood flowing and prevent stiffness.

- **Seated marches:** Lift your knees alternately as if marching while seated to engage your core and legs.

- **Shoulder rolls:** Roll your shoulders forward and backward to relieve tension and improve circulation.

- **Neck stretches:** Gently tilt your head side to side or forward and backward to stretch your neck muscles.

- **Walk the aisles:** Whenever the seatbelt sign is off, take short walks up and down the aisle to stretch your legs and stay active. (*Pro tip: Navigate carefully to avoid turning into a human speed bump for flight attendants or getting caught in the awkward bathroom line shuffle. Bonus points if you make it back to your seat without grabbing every headrest for balance!*)

- **Calf raises:** Stand near your seat and rise onto your toes, holding briefly before lowering yourself. This can help prevent swelling and improve circulation.

In the car: A long road trip doesn't mean you have to skip movement.There are several ways to stay active as both a driver and a passenger. Always prioritize safety, and do these exercises during stops, while pumping gas, or when stopped at a traffic light. Passengers can engage in light exercises such as abdominal contractions, seated knee lifts, and calf or toe raises. Once you reach a rest stop, walk in place or do bodyweight exercises such as push-ups or planks. If you have a jump rope, use it to quickly raise your heart rate. Stretching and staying active will keep you energized and comfortable.

At the hotel: Even if the hotel gym is closed or your Airbnb lacks equipment, a brisk walk during sightseeing can keep you active. You can also do yoga to stay flexible and centered, or take a swim if there's access to a pool or beach. If leaving your room is a challenge, try a quick high-intensity workout in your room— no equipment needed! Anything helps, and staying committed to movement will keep you feeling your best on the road.

Suggestions: Work your way through the following exercises, doing reps of 25-20-15-10 as quickly as possible.

- Burpees

- Sit-ups (full sit-up, not just a crunch)

- Push-ups

- Squat jumps (full 90-degree squat, explode into the air, and land back in the deep squat)

- Tricep dips (using a chair or ledge)

- Mountain climbers

- Plank 45-second

Repeat this circuit four times, reducing the reps by five each time.

Ways to Move at the Office

Sitting for long periods in an office or working remotely, can have serious health consequences. In fact, you may have heard the saying, "Sitting is the new smoking." Studies show that prolonged sitting is linked to weight gain, heart disease, diabetes, high blood pressure, and other chronic conditions, and even raises the risk of premature death by 40%. To combat this, it's crucial to incorporate movement into your daily routine. Even simple stretches, standing, or short walks around the office can drastically improve your health and well-being.

Corporate Wellness Programs

You spend a significant portion of your life at work, so why not incorporate health and well-being while working. A wellness program within your company can assist on ensuring your physical and mental health. If your company doesn't have one, consider starting one by implementing a wellness challenge, introducing healthier snack options, encouraging bike-sharing incentives, or offering gym membership discounts. If your workplace already has a corporate wellness program, here's a big piece of advice—PARTICIPATE!

Remember, implementing exercise during work hours can help you stay motivated! A Harvard study shows that it can enhance creativity, improve memory recall, sharpen focus, and speed up learning. Exercise during work hours elevates performance: employees who worked out during work managed their time better, were more productive, and felt more satisfied with their jobs.

Suggestions: Staying active at your desk.

- **Desk stretches:** Stretch your arms, legs, and back while seated or standing to reduce tension and improve circulation.

- **Seated leg raises:** Lift one leg at a time while seated and hold for a few seconds.

- **Chair squats:** Stand up from your chair and sit back down repeatedly to strengthen your legs and glutes.

- **Walking breaks:** Set a timer to remind yourself to walk for a few minutes every hour.

- **Desk push-ups:** Use the edge of your desk for push-ups to engage your upper body and core.

- **Calf raises:** While standing, lift your heels off the ground, then slowly lower them back down.

- **Standing desk:** If possible, use a standing desk or alternate between sitting and standing throughout the day. Many companies offer adjustable desks for employees, allowing them to switch between sitting and standing positions as needed.

If you're working from home or can talk to HR about offering wellness solutions, you can create mini-workout sessions for your employees or colleagues. Exercises such as stretches, 10-minute bodyweight circuits, or even group yoga classes (via video conference) are great ways to get everyone involved.

Boss Moves & Burpees

For all of my Entrepreneurs, Mommapreneurs, and alike—MOVE, MOVE, MOVE! Being an entrepreneur often means juggling countless responsibilities, which can make finding time for exercise feel impossible. Long hours spent in meetings, managing clients, and building a business can leave little room for physical activity. However, maintaining your health and fitness is crucial not only for your personal well-being but also for the success of your business. Entrepreneurs often underestimate the importance of exercise, but regular movement boosts mental clarity, energy levels, and productivity. With the right mindset and a few practical strategies, you can incorporate exercise into even the busiest of schedules. Remember that one of the benefits of exercise for a business owner is that it supports overcoming obstacles and stress. Wouldn't you want to be sharper and less tense when presenting to "High end Client"

Take 10

One of the most effective ways to prioritize fitness as an entrepreneur is to schedule it just like a meeting. Put exercise on your calendar. It becomes a non-negotiable part of your day. You don't need to dedicate hours at the gym; just a 10 to 30-minute workout will make a huge difference. Remember my previous suggestions of high-intensity interval training (HIIT) or quick bodyweight circuits that can be done from home or the office. These short, intense sessions allow you to maximize your time while reaping the benefits of a full workout. Take time to catch some quick endorphins and make a difference during your busy schedule. Not to say you need an intense daily workout, but even small 1-4 minute intervals throughout the day give benefits.

Still Challenging?

How you use your time is essential for balancing entrepreneurship and exercise. If you find it challenging to carve out dedicated time for fitness, try multitasking. Attach movement to a daily, consistent habit.For instance, use time spent on phone calls or brainstorming sessions to do some light stretching or bodyweight exercises like squats or lunges. You can also take advantage of early mornings or late evenings—times when the demands of your business might be lower—to squeeze in a workout. These small efforts add up and ensure you're taking care of your health even during the busiest times.

Keeping a dedicated workout routine is not only good for your health but it's good for business! Hire a personal trainer if you're a power-hungry entrepreneur because it can teach you the "art of letting go" by delegating control to the personal trainer. Joining a team sport can also teach the art of trusting others with important responsibilities.

Final Thought

Finding time for exercise in a busy schedule requires intention, creativity, and commitment. By prioritizing activities like yoga, cardio, and strength training that offer maximum benefits in minimal time, busy individuals can reap the rewards of regular physical activity without sacrificing other priorities. Embracing innovative exercise trends and integrating movement into daily routines can help entrepreneurs stay healthy, energized, and productive, both in business and in life. So seize the day, dear reader, and embark on a journey of self-discovery and transformation—one step, one breath, one rep at a time. Your body and mind will thank you for it.

CHAPTER 3
Watch Your Mouth

Just like a strong mindset and regular movement are vital to maintaining a healthy life, what we put into our bodies is equally important—especially for busy people. But let's approach this with flexibility rather than rigid rules or judgment. In hectic schedules, it's easy to grab whatever's convenient, but making thoughtful, healthier choices can have a significant impact on your energy and overall well-being. This chapter is all about giving you practical strategies for making better nutritional choices, without guilt or unrealistic expectations. We'll also explore the emotional connections we have to food and how those attachments influence our decisions. Ultimately, it's about finding balance and nourishing your body in ways that support your busy life.

Fast Food, Faster Lives

The pace of life has quickened, and our diets have evolved to keep up. As technology accelerates every aspect of our lives, including work and leisure, the way we feed ourselves has adapted. Fast food, quick meals, and ready-made snacks have surged in popularity to match the speed of today's economy and culture. Convenience has become king, and busy Americans often prioritize quick solutions over mindful eating.

Chef Dion, a friend of mine with over 25 years of experience in the food industry, has witnessed this firsthand in restaurants. She recalls how kitchens used to be filled with fresh ingredients and hands-on cooking. Nowadays, it's all prepackaged—everything from meats to vegetables arrives frozen or preserved. Kitchens have more microwaves than stoves, reflecting how the food industry has shifted toward speed and convenience. This reliance on prepackaged food often means more preservatives and sodium, which can impact overall health.

However, it's not all negative. With global connectivity, we now have access to a broader variety of foods than ever before. Grocery stores are offering more health-conscious options, dedicating aisles to organic, gluten-free, and plant-based products. Healthier choices are becoming more accessible, and the variety available to busy Americans is expanding.

As nutrition continues to evolve, balancing convenience with health is key. The challenge lies in making smart choices within this fast-paced food landscape, opting for nutritious alternatives whenever possible.

Fork Wisely, Live Happily

Keeping awareness of what you eat is essential because it allows you to see where potential pitfalls in your diet may lie. Often, we think we are eating healthily, but small, seemingly insignificant snacks or rushed meals can add up without us realizing it. Tracking what you consume can identify areas for improvement in your nutrition. For example, those quick donuts from the office or the bag of chips grabbed between meetings can easily slip your mind, but recording them helps you see the full picture. It's also a great way to track your progress, allowing you to reflect on where you started and how far you've come.

Food tracking has become incredibly easy, thanks to technology. Numerous apps are available that can assist in monitoring your nutrition with just a few taps on your phone. One of my personal favorites is Noom, which I highly recommend for its simplicity and effectiveness—plus it keeps getting better with new updates. After just a couple of weeks of using it, I was able to see patterns in my eating habits that I hadn't noticed before. The app helps keep me in check when I'm tempted to grab a second cookie (my arch enemy) or mindlessly snack. The goal-setting feature is also fantastic for maintaining focus and creating long-term changes.

Tracking what you eat also holds you accountable to yourself. It's like keeping a journal, but specifically for your nutrition, allowing you to reflect on your habits and make adjustments as needed. Who knows you better than you? Consistently recording your meals and snacks commits you to a healthier lifestyle and ensuring that your choices align with your goals. Over time, this builds self-discipline, making it easier to maintain healthy habits and resist temptations.

Food tracking provides valuable data that can guide your decisions moving forward. If your goal is weight loss, muscle gain, or simply eating more balanced meals, having a record of what you eat helps you make more informed choices. It's not just about counting calories; it's about understanding what fuels your body and how it affects your energy, mood, and overall well-being. With this awareness, you can tailor your nutrition to better support your busy lifestyle while still working towards your health goals.

Tracking? Nobody's Got Time!

Indeed, that is what this book is about. As a busy person, finding time to track every meal can feel overwhelming, but there are simple strategies you can adopt to improve your nutrition without a heavy time commitment. One way is to focus on meal planning and preparation at the beginning of the week. Set aside an hour or two on weekends or during a less hectic day to plan and prepare balanced meals. You don't need to track every ingredient—just ensure you have a mix of lean proteins, healthy fats, vegetables, and whole grains. Prepping meals in advance allows you to grab something healthy on the go, reducing the temptation to make poor choices when you're pressed for time. Remember, apps like Noom make tracking effortless—you can simply snap a photo or scan a barcode, and it logs your meal for you in seconds!

Also, it is helpful to develop consistent eating habits. Instead of tracking every snack or meal, you can simplify by having a rotation of go-to nutritious meals that you enjoy. For example, choose a few healthy breakfasts, lunches, and dinners that you can quickly prepare or pick up. If you know what you're eating most of the time, there's less need to track it. Keeping healthy snacks like nuts, fruits, or yogurt within reach will also help curb unhealthy cravings. Streamlining your food choices and prep can assist in maintaining a healthier diet without the stress of detailed tracking.

Prepare and Plan Before You Slay the World

Sunday Night Meal Prep: Meal prepping before the week starts is a powerful way to maintain healthy eating habits. Since many professionals work Monday through Friday, "Sunday Night Meal Prep" has become a go-to strategy. However, you can adjust this to fit your schedule—whatever day marks the start of your week, dedicate time the day before to plan your meals. Even if you aren't a fan of cooking, spending just 45 minutes to an hour on meal prep sets you up for success. Prepping in advance not only saves time but also ensures you make healthier food choices during busy days.

Grocery List: Walking into a grocery store without a list can lead to buying items you don't need, blowing your budget, or straying from your nutrition goals. Having a well-thought-out grocery list can save both time and money, while also positively affecting your health by keeping you on track. Plan your list based on how many servings you'll need for the week, focusing especially on protein and essential ingredients like spices. Apps can be your friend here—many are designed to help you organize a healthy shopping list, so check out options like AnyList, Mealime, or Paprika to make your trips even easier.

Weekly Calendar: Just like a business relies on record-keeping, your nutrition needs structure and planning. A weekly nutrition calendar can help you stay on track by mapping out what you plan to eat based on your upcoming tasks, meetings, and events. You'll be able to spot potential pitfalls in advance, allowing you to proactively stick to your goals. Plan day-by-day and include meal times, snacks, and hydration to stay consistent throughout the week. This method also helps you avoid unhealthy choices during unpredictable moments that pop up in your schedule.

Batch Cooking: If you're too busy to cook every night, batch cooking is a lifesaver. Set aside time to prepare larger quantities of a few versatile meals that you can portion out and use throughout the week. Think stir-fries, grain bowls, roasted veggies, or even healthy casseroles that you can freeze. This reduces the temptation to grab fast food when you're in a rush and ensures that you always have a nutritious meal waiting for you.

Snack Planning: Snacks are often where people fall off their healthy eating plans, especially during long workdays. Instead of reaching for chips or candy, plan out your snacks just like your meals. Pre-pack small portions of nuts, fruits, yogurt, or veggie sticks so that when hunger strikes, you have a healthy option on hand. This keeps you fueled throughout the day and prevents overeating at mealtime.

These strategies create a solid foundation for maintaining healthy nutrition even when life gets busy. Preparing in advance keeps you consistent and focused on your health goals.

Quality of Food Matters

When it comes to maintaining a healthy weight, many people focus on counting calories, but emerging research suggests that food quality is just as important, if not more so. Instead of simply choosing foods based on caloric value, it's crucial to focus on high-quality, nutrient-dense options. Eating wholesome, unprocessed foods provides essential vitamins, minerals, and energy that your body needs to function properly. Minimizing low-quality, processed foods ensures you are not just feeding yourself but nourishing yourself in a way that supports long-term health. The focus should shift from calorie counting to prioritizing high-quality, healthy foods that fuel your body.

Poor Quality Foods Have Consequences

Poor-quality foods are often highly processed, fried, or loaded with refined sugars and unhealthy fats. Items like chips, cookies, and other vending machine snacks are quick fixes but offer little nutritional value. Regular consumption of these foods can lead to weight gain, increased susceptibility to illness, and a general decline in overall well-being. The body struggles to function optimally when fueled by these low-nutrient options, making it harder to stay healthy. Reducing your intake of these items and replacing them with whole, nutrient-rich foods will make a significant difference in how you feel and perform.

You End Up Eating More

One of the hidden dangers of poor-quality food is that it often leaves you hungry sooner and less satisfied after eating. Processed foods lack the fiber, protein, and healthy fats that keep you feeling full, so you end up eating more throughout the day. This not only leads to consuming more calories than intended but also causes energy crashes, leaving you sluggish and tired. High-quality foods, on the other hand, provide long-lasting energy and help stabilize blood sugar levels, preventing that afternoon slump.

High-Quality Foods Taste Better

One of the best parts of eating healthier, high-quality foods is the incredible flavor they provide. Natural, fresh ingredients often have richer, more complex flavors than processed foods. For instance, I remember trying organic ground turkey for the first time, which was lighter and fresher than the conventional beef I was used to. I was skeptical at first, but after cooking it, the taste blew me away—it was rich, tender, and flavorful. Quality foods are not only better for your health, but they also make meals more enjoyable, turning eating into a delightful experience.

Long-Term Benefits of High-Quality Foods

Eating high-quality foods doesn't just affect your waistline; it impacts your overall health and longevity. A diet rich in fruits, vegetables, lean proteins, and whole grains helps reduce the risk of chronic diseases such as heart disease, diabetes, and even certain cancers. These foods also support brain health, boosting cognitive function and mood. By making mindful decisions about what you eat, you're investing in your future, ensuring that you not only feel great now but are also setting the foundation for a healthier, longer life.

Lifestyle and Diet

Diet is a temporary trend and potentially harmful. Diets are often short-term solutions that promise quick results, especially for specific events like weddings or reunions. While they may help shed pounds rapidly, many diet trends come with extreme restrictions that can do more harm than good. These diets often lack balance, depriving your body of essential nutrients, which can lead to fatigue, muscle loss, and other health issues. Once the diet ends, many people experience rapid weight gain, often regaining more than they initially lost. Diets offer a temporary fix, but they aren't sustainable for long-term health.

Lifestyle is a long-term and sustainable approach. Adopting a healthy lifestyle is a more sustainable and effective way to maintain long-term health and wellness. Unlike diets that come and go, a lifestyle approach is about making gradual, consistent changes to your eating habits. Research shows that small, steady adjustments are more likely to result in lasting health benefits, as your body adapts more positively to slow changes. By focusing on balanced meals, portion control, and moderation, you can create healthy habits that become part of your daily routine without the stress of extreme diets.

Just think of balance and flexibility over restriction. The key difference between a diet and a lifestyle change is balance. A diet often comes with strict rules and limitations, making it difficult to enjoy food and life. A lifestyle change embraces flexibility, allowing room for treats and indulgences without guilt. It promotes a balanced relationship with food, where nutritious choices are a priority but not at the expense of pleasure or enjoyment. For busy people, a lifestyle change is easier to maintain because it fits naturally into the demands of everyday life, making healthy living a lasting habit rather than a fleeting trend.

Nutrition for the Chronically Busy

Take Micro Steps: When it comes to making nutrition a part of your busy lifestyle, it's important to start small. I always emphasize breaking down big tasks into manageable steps, and this is especially true for making lasting nutritional changes. Rather than overhauling your diet all at once, focus on one or two small goals, like reducing soda intake or bringing a healthy lunch twice a week. Once you've mastered those habits over a couple of weeks, add something new, like "Tofu Tuesdays" or increasing your vegetable intake. These micro-steps create a gradual, sustainable shift without overwhelming you, making it easier to maintain long-term.

Observe the Difference: Tracking your progress and reviewing how you feel is crucial when adopting a healthier lifestyle. After each week or month of new changes, take some time to reflect on what worked and what didn't. This self-awareness helps you fine-tune your habits and adjust when something isn't quite working. Keeping a simple food journal can be incredibly useful to analyze your energy levels, digestion, and mood. Not only does this process give you insight into your body's responses, but it also helps you stay motivated as you observe the positive impact of your choices.

Make Short, Short-Term Goals: Setting short-term, achievable goals is a great way to stay on track without feeling overwhelmed. For instance, if your long-term goal is to lose 40 pounds or maintain a healthier diet, break it down into smaller, more manageable chunks. Focus on one week at a time by setting goals like preparing nutritious lunches or cutting out processed snacks. Once you reach these smaller milestones, you'll feel a sense of accomplishment, which fuels your motivation to keep going. Short-term goals make big changes feel more achievable, helping you stick with your healthy habits despite a busy schedule.

Benefits of Enjoying Your Food

I must emphasize that eating nutritious food doesn't have to feel like a chore, even for the busiest people. In fact, when you learn to truly enjoy the food you're consuming, it can make all the difference in maintaining healthy eating habits. With a bit of creativity and intention, nourishing your body can become something you look forward to, rather than a burden. When focusing on delicious, whole foods and allowing yourself to savor each meal, you'll not only fuel your body properly, but also experience mental and emotional satisfaction. Even with a tight schedule, enjoying nutritious food is possible and incredibly rewarding. Huge benefits!

It's in Our Nature: Shifting to a healthier nutrition plan doesn't mean you have to sacrifice flavor or joy. In fact, enjoying your food can help you stick with your healthy changes more effectively. We are naturally wired to appreciate the look, taste, and feel of food, so why not embrace that? There are many ways to make your healthy meals enjoyable, such as growing your own food or cooking with family. These activities not only enhance the flavor but also provide mental and physical health benefits, creating a positive relationship with what you eat.

Prevents Us from Falling Off: When you truly enjoy the food you're eating, you're much less likely to abandon your healthy habits. Cultivating a positive mindset around your nutrition makes it easier to stay consistent. Research shows that if you practice a new habit for 30 days, you're much more likely to make it stick long-term. Involving friends or family in your meals or sharing healthy recipes is also a great way to stay accountable. This combination of enjoyment and support keeps you on track, helping you achieve your nutrition goals.

God Gave Us These Taste Buds for a Reason: It's natural to crave certain foods, especially those introduced to us during childhood. But the good news is that as you reduce unhealthy options like salty or sugary snacks, your taste buds will adjust to healthier foods. Over time, you'll find that you need less salt, sugar, or processed flavors to enjoy your meals. Embrace the full, natural flavors of whole food! You're not only doing your body a favor, but you're also reigniting your love for food in a healthier, more sustainable way.

Making Tough Situations at Work Workable

Work can often present tough situations when it comes to maintaining healthy habits, especially when you're faced with temptations like office snacks, long meetings, or busy schedules. But the key to success is preparation, mindfulness, and small, intentional choices. Just because the work environment might seem to sabotage your healthy goals doesn't mean you have to give in entirely. With a few strategic steps, you can make even the most difficult situations manageable, ensuring that your nutrition stays on track. Here's how to navigate those tough moments while keeping your health in mind.

Step Back: Hesitation can be your best defense when faced with unhealthy options at work. Instead of indulging in poor-quality snacks immediately, take a moment to step back. If you still decide to eat it, consider having it earlier in the day so you can burn off some of those calories during your usual activities. Better yet, try to eat only a portion, or skip it entirely. This simple pause can help you make more mindful choices without feeling deprived.

Munch Prior to: Scheduling your meals or snacks ahead of time is one of the best ways to avoid unhealthy snacking during work hours. If you know you have a long meeting or a busy day ahead, make sure to eat beforehand. Bringing snacks like nuts, fruit, or tea with you can curb hunger during unexpected moments. This will prevent you from grabbing whatever is easily available, which is often unhealthy.

Have Your Arsenal Ready: When faced with common temptations like cookies or sweets brought in by coworkers, having your own healthier options on hand can be a game-changer. Keeping a stash of snacks like yogurt, granola, or nuts gives you an easy, nutritious alternative. And if the pressure to join in is too strong, it's okay to indulge—just try to limit yourself. Research shows that sometimes just a bite or two is enough to satisfy a craving. Also, take it a step further by contributing healthy options for the whole office, like a bowl of fruit or bringing a blender for smoothies. Small changes like these can help foster a healthier work environment for everyone.

Re-emphasis on Mindset with Nutrition

Take on Healthy Nutrition Habits Happily: I encourage you to revisit the chapter on Mindset, as it's essential when approaching any change, especially with nutrition. Your mindset can either set you up for success or make the process feel like a burden. So, ask yourself—are you excited about this new journey, or does it feel like a burden? Approaching your nutritional goals with positivity and excitement will help you stay consistent. See it as an opportunity to nourish your body, not just another task. This way, the process becomes enjoyable, not dreaded.

Accept the Small Failures: Failure is inevitable, and that's okay. Expect that there will be moments when you don't stick to your goals perfectly—whether it's indulging in an unhealthy snack or missing a weight target. Old habits die hard, and it's normal to have setbacks. The key is not to let small failures discourage you from continuing your healthy nutrition journey. Accept the bumps in the road as part of the process and keep moving forward.

Your Health Is Your Business!: For busy professionals, your health is your greatest investment. Just like running a business, your health needs regular attention, strategy, and commitment. When neglected, it can impact your performance and productivity, just as a poorly run business eventually collapses. Making healthy nutritional choices is like investing in your future success—it will give you the energy, focus, and longevity to excel in your career and personal life. Prioritize your health as you would any important business decision.

For busy people, especially those who are career-driven, making nutrition a top priority is vital. I've seen many successful, intelligent women fall victim to poor health, even as they excel in their careers. If we work to eliminate risks like diabetes, cancer, high blood pressure, and heart disease through better nutrition, we can become stronger and more efficient for our clients, colleagues, and ourselves. Prioritizing healthy habits will not only improve your health, but it will also enhance your ability to succeed in all aspects of life.

> *"If you want something new, you have to stop doing something old."*
>
> – Peter Drucker

7 Quick Tips

1. **Meal Plan/Prep Once a Week** – Dedicate time on Sundays or your least busy day to prep meals and snacks for the entire week. This saves time and ensures you always have

something healthy on hand. If you're still too busy, take 10 minutes to make a plan.

2. **Focus More on Whole Foods and Less on Processed** – Opt for whole foods like fruits, veggies, lean proteins, and whole grains over processed or prepackaged options. They're more nutritious and keep you fuller for longer. The more water-dense and less dry, the better.

3. **Pack It Up** – Always carry healthy snacks like almonds, veggies, fruit, or yogurt to avoid vending machine temptations or pressure situations. These quick bites keep your energy stable throughout the day. Keep them in the car, bag, or a convenient spot where you can easily access them.

4. **Water! Water! Water!** – Start your day with a glass of water before anything else and carry a reusable bottle to stay hydrated throughout the day. Water helps with digestion, energy levels, and overall well-being. Swap sugary sodas, energy drinks, or coffee laden with syrups for herbal teas or water. This reduces unnecessary calorie intake and helps stabilize blood sugar levels.

5. **Protein is Power** – Ensure you're getting enough protein at every meal, whether from meat, fish, legumes, or plant-based sources. This helps keep you full and boosts your metabolism.

6. **Mind Your Portions with Highly Dense Foods** – Keep an eye on portion sizes, especially if you eat out often. Consider asking for a half portion or packing half your meal for later to avoid overeating.

7. **Utilize the Slow Cooker** – This is my favorite tip! Utilizing a slow cooker is a game-changer for busy people looking to maintain healthy eating habits, especially if you have children! Simply throw in your ingredients in the morning, and by the time you're done with work, you have a nutritious meal ready to go. Slow cooking allows you to use whole, unprocessed foods like lean meats, veggies, and legumes, which retain their nutrients and flavors over time. Plus, it saves time on meal prep during the week and reduces the temptation to grab fast food on hectic days.

7 Quick 30-Minute Recipes for Super Busy People

Sweet Potato Avo Egg

Ingredients:

- 2 medium sweet potatoes

- 2 large eggs

- 1 ripe avocado

- 1 tablespoon olive oil

- Salt and pepper, to taste

- Optional toppings: red pepper flakes, chopped cilantro, lime juice

Instructions:

1. **Prepare the Sweet Potatoes**: Preheat your oven to 400°F (200°C). Wash and scrub the sweet potatoes, then poke a

few holes in each with a fork. Place them on a baking sheet and bake for about 15-20 minutes, or until fork-tender. Alternatively, you can microwave them for 5-7 minutes until soft.

2. **Cook the Eggs**: While the sweet potatoes are cooking, heat the olive oil in a non-stick skillet over medium heat. Crack the eggs into the skillet and cook them to your liking (sunny-side up, scrambled, or poached). Season with salt and pepper.

3. **Prepare the Avocado**: While the eggs are cooking, cut the avocado in half, remove the pit, and scoop the flesh into a bowl. Mash it lightly with a fork and add a pinch of salt, pepper, and a squeeze of lime juice (optional).

4. **Assemble the Dish**: Once the sweet potatoes are cooked, slice them in half lengthwise. Spread a generous amount of mashed avocado on each half of the sweet potato. Top with the cooked eggs and sprinkle with red pepper flakes and chopped cilantro if desired.

Time: 20 minutes

Quick Spaghetti Squash

Ingredients:

- 1 medium spaghetti squash
- 2 tablespoons olive oil
- Salt and pepper, to taste
- 1 cup cherry tomatoes, halved
- 1 cup fresh spinach
- 2 cloves garlic, minced

- 1 teaspoon Italian seasoning (or to taste)
- 1/4 cup grated Parmesan cheese (optional)
- Fresh basil for garnish (optional)

Instructions:

1. **Prepare the Spaghetti Squash**: Preheat your oven to 400°F (200°C). Carefully cut the spaghetti squash in half lengthwise and scoop out the seeds. Drizzle the inside with 1 tablespoon of olive oil and season with salt and pepper.

2. **Roast the Squash**: Place the squash halves cut-side down on a baking sheet lined with parchment paper. Roast for about 25-30 minutes, or until the flesh is tender and can be easily shredded with a fork.

3. **Sauté the Vegetables**: While the squash is roasting, heat the remaining tablespoon of olive oil in a large skillet over medium heat. Add the minced garlic and sauté for about 1 minute until fragrant. Add the halved cherry tomatoes and spinach, cooking until the spinach is wilted (about 2-3 minutes). Season with Italian seasoning, salt, and pepper.

4. **Combine and Serve**: Once the spaghetti squash is done, use a fork to scrape the flesh into spaghetti-like strands. Add the spaghetti squash strands to the skillet with the sautéed vegetables, tossing to combine. If desired, sprinkle with grated Parmesan cheese and garnish with fresh basil.

Time: 30 minutes

Apples and Almonds Snack

Ingredients:

- 1 medium apple (any variety you prefer)
- 2 tablespoons almond butter (or a handful of raw almonds)
- Optional toppings: cinnamon, honey, or granola

Instructions:

1. **Prep the Apple**: Core and slice the apple into wedges or rounds.

2. **Serve with Almonds**: If using almond butter, place it in a small bowl. If using raw almonds, set them aside.

3. **Add Optional Toppings**: Drizzle honey or sprinkle cinnamon on the apple slices, if desired.

Time: 5 minutes

Versatile Tacos

Ingredients:

- Small corn or whole wheat tortillas
- Lettuce or cabbage
- Tomato
- Cilantro
- Onion
- Salsa
- Lime
- Protein options: skinless chicken breast, lean steak, shrimp, salmon, lean ground beef or turkey, tofu, or black beans.

Instructions:

1. **Prepare the Protein**: In a dry skillet, warm each tortilla for about 30 seconds on each side until soft and pliable. You can also microwave them in a damp paper towel for 15-20 seconds.

2. **Assemble the Tacos**: Lay a tortilla flat and add a portion of your cooked protein of choice. Top with shredded lettuce, diced tomatoes, onion, avocado slices, and cheese if using. Drizzle with salsa or lime juice, if desired. Serve immediately and enjoy your customizable tacos!

Time: 30 minutes

Greek Yogurt Parfait

Ingredients:

- Greek yogurt
- Granola
- Mixed berries
- Chia seeds
- Honey

Instructions:

1. **Layer the Parfait**: Layer Greek yogurt with granola, berries, and chia seeds.

2. **Drizzle with Honey**: Add honey for a quick breakfast or snack.

Time: 5 minutes

Slow Cooker Turkey Chili

Ingredients:

- 1 pound ground turkey (lean)
- 1 can (15 oz) kidney beans, drained and rinsed
- 1 can (15 oz) black beans, drained and rinsed
- 1 can (15 oz) diced tomatoes (with juices)
- 1 can (6 oz) tomato paste
- 1 medium onion, diced
- 1 bell pepper, diced (any color)
- 2 cloves garlic, minced
- 1 cup corn (frozen or canned)
- 2 tablespoons chili powder
- 1 teaspoon cumin
- 1 teaspoon smoked paprika
- Salt and pepper to taste
- 1 cup low-sodium chicken or vegetable broth
- 1 zucchini squash (optional)
- Optional toppings: chopped cilantro, avocado, shredded cheese, or Greek yogurt

Instructions:

1. **Brown the Turkey**: In a skillet over medium heat, brown the ground turkey until fully cooked, breaking it apart with a spoon. Drain any excess fat.

2. **Combine Ingredients in Slow Cooker**: In a slow cooker, combine the cooked turkey, kidney beans, black beans, diced tomatoes, tomato paste, diced onion, bell pepper, garlic, corn, chili powder, cumin, smoked paprika (if using), salt, pepper, and broth.

3. **Cook**: Stir everything together until well mixed. Cover and cook on low for 6 hours or high for 3 hours.

4. **Serve**: Once cooked, taste and adjust seasoning if necessary. Serve hot with your choice of toppings, such as chopped cilantro, diced avocado, shredded cheese, or a dollop of Greek yogurt.

Time: 10 minutes (slow cooker time varies)

Grilled Eggplant Parmesan

Ingredients:

- 1 large eggplant, sliced into 1/2-inch rounds
- 2 tablespoons olive oil
- Salt and pepper to taste
- 1 cup marinara sauce (store-bought or homemade)
- 1 cup part-skim mozzarella cheese, shredded
- 1/4 cup grated Parmesan cheese
- Fresh basil leaves for garnish
- 1 teaspoon Italian seasoning

Instructions:

1. **Preheat the Grill**: Heat your grill to medium-high.

2. **Prepare the Eggplant**: In a large bowl, toss the eggplant slices with olive oil, salt, and pepper. If using, add Italian seasoning for extra flavor.

3. **Grill the Eggplant**: Place the eggplant slices on the grill. Cook for about 5-7 minutes on each side, until tender and grill marks appear. Remove from the grill and set aside.

4. **Assemble the Dish**: In a baking dish, layer the grilled eggplant slices. Spoon a little marinara sauce over each slice, then sprinkle with mozzarella and Parmesan cheese.

5. **Broil (Optional)**: If you prefer melted cheese, you can place the assembled dish under the broiler for about 2-3 minutes until the cheese is bubbly and golden brown. Keep a close eye to avoid burning.

6. **Serve**: Garnish with fresh basil leaves and serve warm.

Time: 30 minutes

Final Thought

Taking control of what you consume is an essential step toward nurturing both your body and mind. It's not about perfection, but about making conscious, compassionate choices that work for you. Embrace flexibility and understand the emotional ties we have to food, we can create a more balanced and mindful approach to nutrition. Whether it's swapping processed snacks for whole foods or simply slowing down to savor each meal, small changes can have a lasting impact. Always remember, it's about progress and nourishing yourself in ways that fuel your energy and support your busy life. With these strategies, you can find a harmonious relationship with food that boosts your well-being and empowers you to thrive.

CHAPTER 4

Check Your Surroundings

This chapter you MUST pay attention too! Your relationships and environment have a profound effect on your well-being. Just as we nurture our physical health with regular exercise and nutritious food, the people and places we surround ourselves with play a crucial role in fostering happiness, growth, and overall health. In this chapter, we'll explore the importance of cultivating a strong support system—whether it's family, friends, work, or the spaces we call home. Making this a healthy habit means being intentional about the energy we allow into our lives, and how we invest in relationships that nourish and empower us. Checking your surroundings, you create a foundation for emotional and mental well-being that supports your journey to a healthier, more balanced life.

Loved Ones: Blood or Emotionally Connected

Family, as the saying goes, is not just important—it's everything. Whether related by blood or emotionally connected, our loved ones often serve as the foundation of our support system. They offer unwavering encouragement, provide a listening ear, and give unconditional love. Plus, they've probably been knowing you for if not all, but most of your life. Their belief in our abilities serves as a constant source of motivation, pushing us forward even during times of adversity.

Friends: Companions in Empathy

Close friends are the family we choose for ourselves. They offer companionship, understanding, and empathy through both life's highs and lows. Their presence validates our experiences and emotions, offering comfort and a sense of belonging. Friends create a safe space where we can express ourselves freely, without fear of judgment, and help us feel understood and supported in ways that few others can.

Mentors: Guiding Lights in the Darkness

Mentors are seasoned individuals who have walked the path we aspire to follow. With their wealth of experience, they provide invaluable guidance, wisdom, and insights. Mentors are not only sources of inspiration but also share their failures along with their successes, imparting lessons that can fast-track our personal and professional growth. Their mentorship accelerates our development and instills the confidence needed to overcome challenges.

Networking Groups: Supportive Communities

Networking groups bring together individuals with similar ambitions, often within our industry or related fields. These communities are fertile grounds for collaboration, knowledge-sharing, and mutual support. By connecting with like-minded individuals, we expand our professional networks, gain fresh perspectives, and find solidarity in our endeavors. The support from these groups propels us toward our goals with renewed vigor and focus.

Creative Avenues: Nurture Expression

Creative spaces, such as hobby groups and artistic communities, encourage self-expression and personal exploration. These environments allow us to unleash our creativity, free from constraints or judgment. The encouragement we receive in these spaces emboldens us to pursue our passions with energy and enthusiasm. Through creative pursuits, we discover new dimensions of ourselves, finding purpose and fulfillment in the process.

Colleagues: Work Advocates

Colleagues play a pivotal role in our professional journey. Through their support and advocacy, they amplify our efforts, helping us make a more significant impact in our work. Their collaboration fosters a culture of success, where mutual respect and recognition flourish. In the workplace, colleagues inspire and encourage us, fueling our ambitions and helping us achieve excellence.

Virtual Systems: Digital Support

This is an interconnected world, virtual systems such as apps, online forums, and virtual reality platforms provide digital support and guidance. These tools connect us to a global community of knowledge and expertise, allowing us to access advice and assistance from anywhere, at any time. Virtual systems serve as lifelines, offering support and resources that keep us grounded and focused on our pursuits.

Educational Resources: Continuous Growth

Educational resources, including books, podcasts, and courses, catalyze continuous learning and growth. These resources expand our understanding and equip us with the skills needed to thrive. The guidance provided by these tools helps propel us toward personal and professional excellence, stimulating a lifelong commitment to self-improvement. In our pursuit of knowledge, we open new doors to opportunity, enriching our lives and broadening our horizons.

Volunteer Organizations: Giving Back and Connecting

Volunteer organizations offer unique opportunities to give back to the community while also forging meaningful connections. Through service, we contribute to the greater good and create lasting bonds with others. The support we receive through volunteer work nourishes our souls, fostering a sense of purpose and fulfillment. In helping others, we boost our own lives with gratitude, compassion, and a deeper sense of community.

Therapist/Counselor: Mental and Emotional Support

Therapists and counselors provide a safe space for introspection and healing, offering professional support for mental and emotional well-being. With their expertise, they help us navigate life's challenges with resilience and clarity. Through their compassionate guidance, we strengthen our inner resolve, gaining the tools needed to confront our fears and insecurities. In therapy, we find both solace and understanding, laying the groundwork for growth and self-discovery.

Healthcare Professionals: Physical Well-Being

Healthcare professionals, such as physicians, dietitians, and trainers, are dedicated to supporting our physical well-being. Their expert guidance empowers us to prioritize health and vitality, nurturing both our bodies and minds. Their advocacy helps us develop healthy habits and lifestyle choices that contribute to long-term wellness. With their support, we lay the foundation for longevity and vitality, guided by a network of committed professionals.

Life Coach: Motivation and Accountability

A life coach offers personalized support and accountability, empowering us to achieve our goals with clarity and purpose. Through their guidance and motivation, they help us push past our limitations and reach new heights of success. Their belief in our potential fuels our determination, helping us unlock our full capabilities and move forward with confidence. In coaching, we discover our strength and resilience, embracing a life full of purpose and passion.

Financial Advisor: Your Finances

A financial advisor provides essential guidance in managing our finances, helping us build a secure and prosperous future. They offer expert advice on complex financial decisions, empowering us to make informed choices that ensure long-term success. With their help, we optimize our resources and work toward financial freedom, confident in the knowledge that we are being guided by a trusted expert.

The Support System: Threads That Bind Us

Support systems are the threads that bind us together, guiding us through the twists and turns of our personal and professional journeys. Whether from loved ones, friends, mentors, or professionals, the encouragement and wisdom we receive empower us to reach our fullest potential. Keen to focus on a strong network of support, we lay the foundation for a life filled with purpose, passion, and fulfillment. Let us cherish and nurture these connections, for it is through them that we find the strength, courage, and clarity to chase our dreams and conquer our fears.

Work Environment: A Place of Growth or Burnout?

You spend a significant portion of your life at work, so your professional environment plays a major role in your mental and physical health. A supportive work environment fosters collaboration, respect, and opportunities for growth. It allows you to succeed, reach your full potential, and feel a sense of purpose in what you do.

However, a toxic workplace can have the opposite effect, leading to burnout, stress, and even physical health problems. If your work environment is filled with negativity, excessive pressure, or a lack of support, it's important to recognize these issues and take steps to address them. If it's setting boundaries with demanding colleagues or exploring new career opportunities, your work life should contribute to your well-being, not detract from it.

Home Life: Your Sanctuary or Source of Stress?

Your home should be your sanctuary—a place where you can relax, recharge, and feel safe. But if your home environment is cluttered, chaotic, or filled with conflict, it can become a source of stress. A disorganized or tense home can contribute to anxiety, feelings of overwhelm, and even affect your sleep and overall mood.

Take a moment to evaluate your living space. Is it a reflection of peace and comfort, or does it feel more like a steel chain? Consider decluttering, creating spaces for relaxation, and addressing any unresolved conflicts within your household. A calm, organized, and supportive home environment can significantly improve your mental and emotional health.

The Ripple Effect of Surroundings on Health

Your surroundings don't just affect your mood or mindset—they also have a direct impact on your physical health. Chronic stress caused by toxic relationships, an unhealthy work environment, or a chaotic home life can lead to conditions like hypertension, headaches, and even weakened immunity. On the other hand, a nurturing and supportive environment can lower stress levels, boost your immune system, and enhance overall vitality.

Healthy environments and relationships promote healthy habits. When you're surrounded by positive influences, you're more likely to engage in activities that support your well-being, such as regular exercise, healthy eating, and mindfulness practices. A positive support system can also encourage you to seek help when you need it, whether that's professional counseling, medical advice, or simply a listening ear.

How to Build a Supportive Environment

Building a healthy support system takes time and effort, but the rewards are invaluable. Here are a few steps to help you create an environment that nurtures your well-being:

- **Assess Your Relationships:** Regularly evaluate the quality of your relationships. Are they supportive and uplifting, or do they create stress and negativity? Be honest about which connections serve your well-being and which may need to be adjusted.

- **Set Boundaries:** HUGE! Don't be afraid to set boundaries with people who drain your energy or negatively impact your well-being. It's okay to limit time with certain individuals or establish clear guidelines for how you want to be treated.

- **Seek Out Positive Influences:** Surround yourself with people who inspire and support you. This may mean expanding your social circle to include more like-minded individuals who share your values and goals.

- **Create a Healthy Home Environment:** Take steps to make your home a place of peace and comfort. Declutter your space, create designated areas for relaxation, and address any unresolved conflicts that may be affecting the harmony of your household.

- **Enhance Your Work Life:** If your job is a source of stress, look for ways to improve your work environment. This could involve setting boundaries with colleagues, seeking professional development opportunities, or even exploring a career change if necessary.

- **Prioritize Self-Care:** Your surroundings include the time and space you dedicate to yourself. Make sure you prioritize self-care by creating routines that support your mental, emotional, and physical health.

Final Thought

Your surroundings have the power to shape your life in profound ways. Be consciously, steadfast at building a supportive network of relationships. Creating a positive home and work environment, and prioritizing your well-being, you can gain an environment that allows you to blossom. Take the time to check your surroundings regularly and make adjustments where needed, ensuring that your support system nourishes your health, happiness, and growth. This also maybe be where your time is wasted or more productive!

CHAPTER 5

Press Pause

Life has a way of sweeping us into a whirlwind of endless to-do lists, meetings, chores, and responsibilities. It feels like there's always something vying for your attention, leaving little room to catch your breath. But here's the thing—just like your phone, your brain and body need to recharge, too. You wouldn't expect your phone to last all day on 1% battery, so why do the same to yourself? This chapter is all about hitting the pause button, whether that means getting quality rest, taking intentional breaks, or simply stopping to refocus. Let's dive into the art (and science!) of pausing.

The Case for Pausing: Why It Matters

First, let's talk about why pressing pause is so crucial. Pausing isn't about being lazy or unproductive; it's about creating space to breathe, reflect, and recharge. When you rest, your body repairs itself, your brain organizes information, and your soul gets a chance to stretch. Without these moments, you risk burnout, reduced creativity, and even health issues like anxiety, high blood pressure, and weakened immunity. So, if you think you're too busy to take a break, remember this: Rest is not a luxury—it's a necessity.

Sleep: Your Body's Magic Reset Button

Sleep is the ultimate form of pausing, and let's be real, most of us aren't getting enough of it. Adults need about 7-9 hours of sleep per night, but how many of us actually hit that target? Sleep is when your body gets to work behind the scenes—repairing tissues, boosting your immune system, and consolidating memories. It's like your brain's overnight cleaning crew, tidying up so you're ready to tackle the next day.

But think about it—many of us are sleep-deprived zombies just stumbling through the day! Don't worry, though—we've got the ultimate guide to help you unlock the mysteries of sleep, from the coolest gadgets and soothing sounds to surprising benefits and quirky sleep destinations. Ready to become a sleep ninja? Let's dive in!

Nature's Free Superpower with Benefits!

More Energy and Alertness: A good night's sleep leaves you feeling energized and alert throughout the day. When combined with activity, quality sleep improves engagement and boosts your daily energy by restoring and rebuilding cells.

Counters Stress: Sleep is your body's stress-processing time. Without enough rest, your body enters a stress state, leading to high blood pressure and increased production of stress hormones, which can disrupt sleep further and increase health risks.

Live Longer: According to the British Whitehall Study, getting adequate sleep reduces the risk of cardiovascular disease. Those who sleep less than five hours are 12% more likely to die prematurely than those who get eight hours of sleep.

Bad Sleep: Your Worst Nightmare

We all love a good nightmare—when it's just a movie. But what if your real-life nightmare is simply not getting enough sleep? Bad sleep turns you into a zombie, a grump, and maybe even a snackaholic searching for energy in all the wrong places. From forgetfulness to mood swings (and let's not even talk about those under-eye bags), poor sleep is the plot twist you don't want. So, let's dive into why bad sleep is truly your worst nightmare—and how to wake up from it!

Weakened Immune System: Sleep deprivation reduces the production of cytokines, proteins essential for fighting inflammation and infection. This weakens your immune system, making it harder to battle illnesses.

Brain Fog and Cognitive Decline: Poor sleep affects memory, cognition, creativity, and the brain's ability to clear toxins. Chronic sleep deprivation has also been linked to depression and Alzheimer's disease.

Aging and Appearance: Sleep deprivation can visibly age you, causing red, puffy eyes, dark circles, and wrinkles. Without proper rest, your skin lacks the time to repair and rejuvenate, leaving it dull and unhealthy. A la we truly do need our beauty rest!

Blue Light: The Real Boogeyman

We've all been there—promising ourselves "just one more episode" or "a quick scroll" before bed, only to find ourselves wide-eyed at 2 AM, deep into conspiracy theory videos or an online debate. Swipe with caution, screens are the ultimate sleep thieves, and they don't even wear masks.

Stimulating the Brain: Screens, such as phones and monitors, keep your brain active and engaged, which is counterproductive for sleep. Scrolling through social media or reading emails before bed delays the onset of sleep.

Disrupting REM Sleep: The emotional engagement from screen time interferes with REM sleep, the deep restorative phase. Blue light from screens also tricks your brain into thinking it's daytime, suppressing melatonin production and keeping you awake.

Time Takers: This book is about saving time and screens are a black hole for time. What starts as "five minutes" somehow turns into an entire time-travel experience, leaving you wondering where your evening (and sleep) disappeared to.

Track Zzz like a Boss

Tracking your sleep has never been easier, thanks to modern technology. Many of us aren't getting enough rest, but there are devices designed to help improve sleep quality. From wake-up lamps to wearable devices and apps that monitor your sleep patterns and recommend ways to snooze more effectively, you have plenty of tools at your disposal.

Top Sleep Apps

1. Calm – Offers sleep stories, meditation, and soothing soundscapes to help you drift off faster.

2. Headspace – Features guided meditations and sleepcasts designed to quiet your mind.

3. Sleep Cycle – Tracks your sleep patterns and wakes you up during the lightest sleep phase.

4. Pillow – A smart app that analyzes your sleep cycle and

integrates seamlessly with Apple devices.

5. Relax Melodies – Allows you to mix your own soothing sleep soundtracks.

6. Noisli – Creates customizable white noise for better focus, relaxation, or sleep.

7. Rain Rain Sleep Sounds – Provides over 100 natural and ambient sounds to lull you to sleep.

8. Loóna – Combines sleep-inducing activities like storytelling, puzzles, and breathing exercises.

Best Sleep Trackers

1. Fitbit Versa 4 – Monitors sleep stages, heart rate, and provides a Sleep Score for daily insights.

2. Oura Ring – Tracks deep sleep, REM cycles, and overall recovery with pinpoint accuracy.

3. Apple Watch (My Go To)– Built-in Sleep app measures time asleep and heart rate while syncing with iOS apps.

4. Withings Sleep Analyzer – Tracks sleep cycles and even detects potential sleep apnea.

5. Whoop 4.0 – A strap-based tracker that monitors recovery, including sleep performance.

6. Google Nest Hub (2nd Gen) – Offers non-wearable sleep tracking with advanced motion sensors.

7. Muse S – A headband that tracks brain activity and offers guided meditation for better sleep.

8. SleepScore Max – Uses sonar technology to measure your sleep environment and habits.

Sleep Apnea and PAP Therapy:

If your sleep issues go beyond occasional restlessness and verge into insomnia or sleep apnea, consulting a sleep therapist is a must. Sleep apnea, characterized by interrupted breathing during sleep, can be treated with devices like CPAP (Continuous Positive Airway Pressure). These PAP therapy devices ensure comfort, monitor sleep patterns, and provide insights to improve sleep quality. You might look like an elephant but you'll sleep like a baby!

Your Sleep Partner:

The person sleeping beside you—or even in the next room—can be a helpful resource for tracking your sleep. If they wake you up due to loud snoring (definitely my husband), fidgeting, or gasping, it might be a sign of sleep issues that need attention. They can also help track how many hours of actual sleep you're getting. They're right there, so why not let them earn their keep by tracking your sleep?

Sleep Aids that Work, No Sheep Required:

Counting sheep is so last century. If you're still relying on fluffy farm animals to lull you to sleep, it's time for an upgrade! From soothing sounds to cozy pillows, there's a whole arsenal of sleep aids that actually get the job done—no baa-ing required. Ready to sleep like a boss? Here's some game-changers that'll have you snoozing soundly in no time!

Sounds:

White and pink noise are particularly effective for sleep. White noise, like the hum of an air conditioner or fan, evenly distributes sound energy. A friend of mine would also use a blow dryer! Pink noise, with a deeper tone, is equally beneficial in masking distractions like traffic noise.

Comfortable Sleeping Arrangements:

Waking up feeling like a pretzel is not the goal. Take a moment to evaluate your sleeping position (yes, starfishing counts), and consider upgrading to a high-quality mattress. A good sleep surface can be huge, helping to reduce discomfort, improve sleep quality, and prevent you from waking up feeling like you just wrestled a bear in your dream. Prefer plush, firm, or the feels of sleeping on a cloud? Investing in the right setup can take you from midnight Cirque du Soleil performer to Certified Snooze Expert—because flipping around like a rotisserie chicken all night is not a sleep strategy.

Clothing Choices:

What you wear—or don't wear—can make or break your sleep quality. Loose, breathable cotton pajamas are a great choice for staying comfy and cool, while tight-fitting clothes can leave you feeling like a burrito wrapped a little too tight. If you really want to maximize relaxation, ditching clothes altogether might be the way to go! Sleeping in the nude allows for unrestricted movement, better temperature regulation, and hey—it might just earn you some bonus points with your sleep partner. So whether you're team cozy PJs or full-on au naturel, the key is to find what helps you drift off into dreamland with ease.

Sleep Tight, Travel Right:

Traveling is the ultimate test of your ability to sleep anywhere, anytime, and in the weirdest positions. From attempting to curl up in a tiny airplane seat that feels more like a medieval torture device, to napping in the back of a bus while trying not to fall onto your fellow passengers, getting a good night's sleep on the road is challenging. Fear not—good sleep while traveling isn't just for the elite few who can fall asleep in 30 seconds on a plane. With a little planning, the right tricks, and maybe some strategically packed snacks, you too can sleep tight and travel right.

Good Sleep and Travel Matters

Circadian Rhythm: Traveling, especially across time zones, disrupts your internal 24-hour clock, or circadian rhythm. Practicing good sleep habits while traveling helps minimize disruptions and keeps your body aligned with its natural sleep-wake cycle.

Reducing Stress: Good sleep reduces travel stress, ensuring you're alert and less irritable during your journey. Proper rest can transform a stressful trip into a pleasurable experience.

Safety on the Road: Sleep deprivation impairs judgment and reaction time, similar to alcohol intoxication. Studies show being awake for 24 hours has effects comparable to a 0.10 blood alcohol level, above the legal driving limit of 0.08.

Rest and Travel Quick Tips

The Travel Pillow, Your Cloud: Packing a travel pillow might feel like a luxury, but trust me, it's your ticket to a better nap. It's not just a fluffy cushion; it's a tiny piece of heaven for your head.

Hydrate, but Not Right Before Bed: While staying hydrated is key, drinking water right before you sleep can turn you into a midnight bathroom sprinter. You'll be tiptoeing down airplane aisles or running to the hotel lobby constantly. Drink enough to stay hydrated, but maybe skip the water chugging contest right before you hit the pillow.

Use Your Headphones: Remember when you tried to sleep with the sound of a crying baby, snoring neighbor, or the constant hum of airplane engines? The pain is real! Enter: noise-canceling headphones. They're like a force field for your ears. Slip them on, pretend you're in your own little world, and suddenly, it's just you and dreamland—no interruptions.

Adjust to the Time Zone... Kinda: When crossing time zones, your body might have a mini panic attack. Don't worry, you don't need to fully embrace the new time zone right away—just start shifting your sleep schedule gradually. Also, try and sleep like it's your first night back home. As long as you're getting some shut-eye, you're winning!

Embrace the Power Nap: Not all sleep needs to happen in a bed. Get yourself cozy in a waiting area, throw on your favorite music, and take a 20-minute power nap. You won't wake up feeling like a grumpy monster, and you'll be ready to tackle your next flight or sightseeing adventure without regrets. Trust me, a power nap is the true "travel hack—I've learned to love it!

Good Sleeping Rest Spots

Finding a good resting spot while traveling is essential for staying refreshed and alert. Whether you're at an airport, in a car, or exploring a new city, choosing a safe and comfortable place to sleep is key. Look for quiet, well-lit areas with security presence if you're in a public space, and always keep your belongings secure to avoid theft. If you're resting in a vehicle, ensure it's parked in a safe location. Prioritizing both comfort and safety will help you get the rest you need without unnecessary stress.

Secluded and Dark Spaces: Choose a space that is quiet, dark, and set to an optimal temperature (60–67°F). Use earplugs, blackout curtains, or a sleep mask to create a calming environment.

Beyond the Bed: You don't always need a bed for quality rest. Take advantage of spots like a secluded office, a conference room, or even your car for a quick nap.

Sleep Destinations: Hotels and travel spots now offer unique sleep-focused experiences, from sleep pods to underwater bedrooms. Adding a sleep destination to your travel plans can make rest more exciting and beneficial.

New Thoughts on Sleep

More Benefits Than Previously Thought: Recent studies reveal that too much sleep (over 9 hours) can lead to heart issues, while proper sleep improves weight management and athletic performance. Sleep also plays a vital role in maintaining healthy organ functions and regulating blood sugar levels.

Social Impact: Sleep deprivation affects your social life, making you more likely to exhibit signs of anxiety and loneliness. People who are well-rested are perceived as more approachable and attractive.

Economic Impact: Sleep deprivation costs economies billions annually in lost productivity and health expenses. In the U.S., it accounts for 1.2 million lost workdays every year, significantly impacting the workforce.

Suggestions: Improve your sleep game

- **Set a Sleep Schedule:** Go to bed and wake up at the same time every day, even on weekends. Your body loves consistency.

- **Create a Sleep Sanctuary:** Keep your bedroom cool, dark, and quiet. And yes, that means no scrolling through TikTok at 2 AM.

- **Wind Down:** Develop a bedtime routine that signals to your brain it's time to chill. Think reading, meditating, or sipping herbal tea.

- **Turn off the Screens:** Blue light from phones and computers messes with your melatonin production. Power down at least an hour before bed.

The Power of Micro-Breaks

Let's move on to daytime pauses—those little moments where you can hit reset without disrupting your entire day. Micro-breaks are short pauses, usually 5-10 minutes, that can make a world of difference in your focus and energy levels. Think of them as mini power-ups for your brain.

Here are some fun ways to take a micro-break:

- **Dance Party for One:** Put on your favorite song and dance like no one's watching. Because, well, no one is.

- **Stretch It Out:** Stand up, reach for the ceiling, touch your toes, and roll your shoulders. Your body will thank you.

- **Go Outside:** Step out for some fresh air and sunlight. Even a quick walk around the block can work wonders.

- **Hydration Station:** Use your break to drink some water or make a cup of tea. Staying hydrated keeps your brain sharp.

Stopping to Refocus: The Art of the Mindful Pause

Sometimes, life feels like a runaway train, and the only way to regain control is to stop, take a deep breath, and refocus. Mindful pauses are about being present in the moment and tuning into what's really important. They're like hitting the refresh button on your mental browser.

Here's how to do it:

- **Breathe:** Take a few slow, deep breaths. Inhale for four counts, hold for four counts, and exhale for six counts. It's a simple way to calm your nervous system.

- **Check In:** Ask yourself, "What do I need right now?" Maybe it's a snack, a nap, or just a moment of quiet.

- **Refocus:** Write down your top three priorities for the day. Let go of what's not urgent or important.

- **Gratitude Break:** Think of three things you're grateful for in that moment. It's a quick mood booster.

Meditation vs. Rest: Same Zen, or Just Pretend?

Sleep is an unconscious state where distractions are removed, allowing your body to recharge. It's a natural state where your mind and body rejuvenate, leaving you refreshed upon waking. Meditation, on the other hand, is a conscious state of heightened awareness and calm. While you may be seated or lying down with your eyes closed, you are fully awake and present. Meditation connects you with your inner self or a higher energy, offering deep relaxation that some mistake for sleep.

Where They Come Together

Both sleep and meditation are hypometabolic states, reducing bodily activities like breathing. While sleep is essential for overall health, meditation supplements it by enhancing mental clarity and reducing stress, providing additional benefits for your body and mind.

Resting Isn't Wasting Time

Raise your hand if you've ever felt guilty for resting. Society has a way of making us feel like we need to hustle 24/7 to be successful, but let's bust that myth right now. Resting isn't wasting time; it's an investment in your well-being and productivity. When you take time to rest, you come back stronger, sharper, and more creative.

Think of rest as a spectrum. On one end, you have full-on sleep, and on the other, you have active rest—like taking a walk, reading a book, or doing yoga. Both are valuable, and the key is to find what works for you.

Practical Ways to Incorporate Pauses into Your Life

If you're ready to make pausing a regular part of your routine, here are some practical ideas to get started:

- **Schedule It:** Block out time in your calendar for rest and reflection. Treat it like any other important appointment.

- **Set Alarms:** Use alarms or reminders to prompt you to take breaks throughout the day.

- **Batch Tasks:** Group similar tasks together so you can focus intensely and then reward yourself with a break.

- **Unplug:** Designate tech-free times or zones in your home to create a sense of calm.

- **Delegate:** Remember, you don't have to do it all. Delegate tasks where you can free up some breathing room.

The Science Behind Pausing

Let's nerd out for a moment. Studies show that pausing boosts productivity, creativity, and decision-making. When you take a break, your brain's default mode network (DMN) kicks in. This network is responsible for daydreaming, problem-solving, and creative thinking. So, those "aha!" moments you have in the shower? That's your DMN at work.

Pausing also helps lower cortisol levels (the stress hormone) and increases dopamine (the feel-good chemical). It's like a mini spa day for your brain.

The Joy of Doing Nothing

Let's talk about dolce far niente—an Italian phrase that means "the sweetness of doing nothing." In our go-go-go culture, the idea of doing nothing can feel revolutionary. But sometimes, the best thing you can do is, well, nothing at all. Sit on the couch, stare out the window, or lie in the grass and watch the clouds. Embrace the stillness and let your mind wander. You might be surprised at how refreshed you feel afterward.

Reflection: The Mental Reset

Pausing isn't just about resting your body; it's also about resetting your mind. Use your breaks to reflect on where you are and where you're going. Ask yourself questions like:

- What's working well in my life right now?

- What's causing me stress, and how can I address it?

- Am I spending my time on things that truly matter to me?

Journaling your thoughts can be a great way to process your reflections and track your progress over time.

Final Thought

Life isn't a sprint; it's a marathon, and even marathon runners need water breaks. When learning to press pause, you give yourself the gift of sustained health, clarity, and joy. So, the next time you feel overwhelmed, remember: It's okay to slow down. Take a breath, take a break, and trust that pausing will help you move forward with more energy and focus. And hey, maybe even throw in a dance party or a nap while you're at it. You've earned it!

CHAPTER 6

Work with What You Got

Life moves fast. Between meetings, deadlines, and family responsibilities, staying healthy can often feel like an impossible mission. One of the reasons why you gave time to this book! The good news: You don't need a personal chef, a home gym, or endless hours of free time to maintain a healthy lifestyle. What you do need is the ability to work with what you've got!

In this chapter, we'll explore how to use the tools right at your fingertips—literally. There are opportunities that you potentially already have that can assist in charging up your wellness. No matter where life takes you, you can stay on track by using what's available. Once you learn how to maximize the resources you already have, living a healthy, balanced life becomes less of a drag and more of a lifestyle. Let's discover how to work smarter—not harder—on your health journey.

Using Technology to Track: Save Time Without Sacrificing Results

Time is precious, especially when life feels like a constant race. The good news? Technology can transform your health journey from overwhelming to efficient with just a few taps on your phone.

Here's how using tech to track your health can save you time while keeping you accountable and motivated:

Instant Post

Gone are the days of writing down every meal or workout in a journal. Health and fitness apps allow you to log meals, workouts, and even water intake instantly. Snap a picture of your meal, select items from a database, and let the app handle the rest. Many apps even offer barcode scanners for packaged foods, making nutrition tracking as simple as grocery shopping.

Instant Record

Your phone can be your personal health assistant. Smartwatches, fitness trackers, and health apps automatically record steps, heart rate, and even sleep patterns—all while you go about your day. There's no need to remember stats or jot anything down—your progress is tracked effortlessly, helping you stay informed and on target.

Instant Measurement

Need to check your running pace, calorie burn, or even hydration levels? There's an app or wearable for that. These tools provide real-time feedback, helping you adjust your efforts instantly. Whether you're crushing a workout or staying mindful of your daily movement, instant measurements keep you informed without taking extra time out of your day.

These technologies to track your health, can eliminate guesswork, save time, and stay on top of your wellness goals—even on your busiest days. It's like having a personal coach, nutritionist, and accountability partner all rolled into one—available whenever and wherever you need it.

Podcasts: Learn, Laugh, and Level Up Anywhere

One of the easiest ways to stay informed, entertained, and inspired—back to mindset conditioning, while on the move is by listening to podcasts. When you're commuting, traveling, or squeezing in a quick walk, podcasts turn idle moments into valuable learning or entertainment time. Here are some top picks across health, economics, and entertainment to keep you engaged while on the go:

Health Podcasts

Stay motivated and learn practical tips to improve your well-being.

- *"The Doctor's Pharmacy"* with Dr. Mark Hyman – A deep dive into functional medicine and holistic health.

- *"The Mind Pump"* – Unfiltered fitness advice with expert insights on workouts and wellness.

- *"Feel Better, Live More"* with Dr. Rangan Chatterjee – Simple lifestyle changes for better health and happiness.

Economic Podcasts

Keep up with the latest financial trends and economic insights.

- *"The Indicator from Planet Money"* – Bite-sized episodes explaining key economic topics in an easy-to-understand way.

- *"Freakonomics Radio"* – Discover how economics shapes everyday life with fascinating stories and data-driven analysis.

- *"The Dave Ramsey Show"* – Financial advice on budgeting, saving, and getting out of debt.

Entertainment Podcasts

Unwind, laugh, and enjoy great stories on the go.

- *"SmartLess"* – Hilarious celebrity interviews hosted by Jason Bateman, Sean Hayes, and Will Arnett.

- *"Pop Culture Happy Hour"* – Reviews and discussions about the latest in TV, film, and pop culture.

- *"The Moth"* – True stories told live that are moving, funny, and unforgettable.

In the mood for health tips, financial advice, or a good laugh, there's a podcast out there ready to keep you company—anytime, anywhere.

There's an App for That: Save Time with Smart Tools

Apps aren't just for fun—they're time-saving tools that can simplify your life. Maybe you're planning a trip, managing a packed schedule, or staying on top of your health, the right app can be a game-changer. Here are some top picks to keep you organized, efficient, and on track:

App for Travel

Plan, book, and explore without the hassle.

- *Google Maps* – Navigate like a pro with real-time traffic updates, directions, and nearby recommendations.

- *Hopper* – Find the best deals on flights and hotels with price predictions and alerts.

- *TripIt* – Organize your travel itinerary in one place, from flights to hotel bookings and rental cars.

App for Time Management

Stay organized, focused, and productive.

- *Trello* – Manage tasks and projects with customizable boards and checklists.

- *Todoist* – Create simple to-do lists and get reminders to stay on top of your tasks.

- *Google Calendar* – Schedule meetings, set reminders, and sync your calendar across devices.

App for Health

Track fitness, nutrition, and mindfulness with ease.

- *MyFitnessPal* – Count calories, track workouts, and log meals with a massive food database.

- *Headspace* – Practice guided meditation and mindfulness to reduce stress and improve focus.

- *FitOn* – Access free workout videos for everything from yoga to HIIT sessions, led by top trainers.

AI: Your 24/7 Health Hack

We have to mention AI, the super duper game changer! The circus of life, you're juggling work, family, and about ten other things—who has time to plan healthy meals or remember to meditate? That's where AI apps like ChatGPT come in! Need a 10-minute workout? Boom, here's a quick routine. Want a meal plan that won't leave you hangry? Done. Looking for stress-busting tips between meetings? You got it. Think of AI as your virtual assistant who never sleeps (so you can). It's like having a personal coach, nutritionist, and sanity saver—all in your pocket, minus the guilt trips. Definitely the topic of my next book!

By using these apps, you can simplify everyday tasks, stay organized, and make progress toward your goals—all while saving valuable time. Let your smartphone do the heavy lifting, so you can focus on what really matters.

Fashionably Fit: Wearable Health Tech

Why not let what you wear do more than just make you look good? Wearable technology has come a long way, helping you stay healthy, track progress, and save time—all while you go about your day. From smartwatches to tech-infused clothing, here are some top wearable gadgets that make multitasking effortless:

Smartwatches: Track health, manage notifications, and stay connected.

- *Apple Watch* – A powerhouse for fitness tracking, heart rate monitoring, and even sending messages—all from your wrist.

- *Garmin Forerunner* – Designed for athletes, it tracks GPS routes, training stats, and even recovery times.

- *Fitbit Versa* – A budget-friendly option for tracking workouts, sleep patterns, and daily steps.

Smart Clothing: Turn your outfit into a fitness tool.

- *Nadi X Smart Yoga Pants* – Built-in sensors gently vibrate to correct your yoga posture.

- *Athos Training Gear* – Smart shirts and shorts track muscle activity and performance during workouts.

- *Polar Team Pro Shirt* – Monitors heart rate, movement, and effort—great for athletes and trainers.

Smart Headgear: Enhance your workout or mindfulness with high-tech headgear.

- *AfterShokz Bone Conduction Headphones* – Deliver music through your cheekbones, leaving your ears open for situational awareness during outdoor runs or bike rides.

- *Muse Headband* – A meditation headband that tracks brain activity and provides real-time feedback to improve mindfulness.

- *Halo Sport 2* – Uses neurostimulation to boost focus and accelerate workout gains.

Smart Jewelry: These pieces give sleek and stylish with your health too.

- *Oura Ring* – Tracks sleep, activity, heart rate, and even readiness for the day.

- *McLear RingPay* – Not a health tracker but a smart ring that enables contactless payments, reducing germ exposure.

- *Ringly* – Smart rings and bracelets that track movement, mindfulness, and phone notifications.

Get Smart! These wearables do more than track—they actively support your health while saving time. Whether you're training for a marathon or managing your busy schedule, wearable tech keeps you connected, informed, and ready for whatever the day brings.

Skip the Trip, Click Instead!

Thankfully, online delivery services make it easier than ever to check tasks off your to-do list without leaving the comfort of your home. From groceries to meal kits and retail goods, these services simplify life and give you back precious time. Here's how:

Grocery Shopping: Skip the store and have fresh ingredients delivered to your door.

- *Instacart* – Order groceries from your favorite local stores with same-day delivery.

- *Amazon Fresh* – Shop a wide range of groceries and essentials with fast delivery options.

- *Walmart Delivery* – Groceries, household items, and more delivered directly from your nearest Walmart.

Meal Prep & Cooking: Spend less time cooking and more time enjoying meals.

- *HelloFresh* – Pre-portioned ingredients and recipes delivered weekly for easy, home-cooked meals.

- *Blue Apron* – Gourmet-inspired meal kits that simplify dinner prep.

- *Freshly* – Fully cooked, healthy meals delivered ready to heat and eat in minutes.

Retail Stores: Get what you need without stepping foot in a store.

- *Amazon Prime* – Everything from gadgets to home essentials with fast, often same-day delivery.

- *Target Drive Up & Delivery* – Order online and choose between home delivery or curbside pickup.

- *Best Buy* – Tech products delivered quickly, often with setup and installation services included.

Letting online delivery services handle shopping, cooking, and errands, you'll free up valuable time for what matters most—

whether it's family, fitness, or taking a well-deserved break. Why spend time running errands? Tech to it!

Desk Job, But Make It Fit

Even with a busy workday, small changes at the office can boost productivity, maintain your health, and save time. From wearable tech to ergonomic adjustments, here's how to work smarter while staying well:

Use Smartwatches: Stay on track without disrupting your workflow.

- **Set Reminders & Alerts** – Get reminders to stretch, drink water, or take short walks.

- **Track Activity** – Record steps, heart rate, and stress levels throughout the day.

- **Manage Notifications** – Stay updated on important calls or messages without constantly checking your phone.

Use Your Cellphone Wisely: Turn your phone into a productivity hub.

- **Task Management Apps** – Stay organized with tools like Trello, Todoist, or Asana.

- **Virtual Meetings** – Join video calls or conferences via Zoom or Microsoft Teams.

- **Health Breaks** – Reset your mind and body with guided meditation apps like Headspace or StretchIt.

Ergonomic Practices: Optimize your workspace for comfort and efficiency.

- **Ergonomic Chair & Desk** – Invest in adjustable furniture to reduce back strain.

- **Keyboard & Mouse Setup** – Use wrist-friendly tools to prevent strain.

- **Blue Light Glasses** – Minimize eye strain during long screen hours.

Embrace Remote Work: Flexibility can enhance productivity.

- **Home Office Setup** – Create a dedicated workspace to maintain focus and work-life balance.

- **Flexible Hours** – Adjust your schedule to work during peak productivity times.

- **Virtual Collaboration Tools** – Streamline communication with platforms like Slack or Google Workspace.

Incorporating these tech tools and office adjustments, you'll maximize productivity while staying healthy and comfortable—all without sacrificing valuable time.

Travel Smart, Stay Healthy: Saving Time on the Go

Traveling can be exciting, but it often brings hectic schedules, delays, and challenges to maintaining wellness. Here's the good news: With thoughtful planning and a proactive mindset, you can stay healthy, save time, and even enjoy your journey more.

Hotel Hacks & Plane Ride Prep

Whether you're at a hotel, Airbnb, or gearing up for a flight, you can maintain your health and routine with simple strategies. Feel free to review the Movement and Nutrition chapters as well!

Hotel or Airbnb: Transform your accommodation into a mini wellness retreat:

- **Use the Furniture**

  - *Chair & Bed Frame Workouts – Perform tricep dips, incline push-ups, or step-ups using sturdy furniture.*

  - *Wall Workouts – Try wall-sits, balance exercises, or stretches to relieve tension.*

- **Maximize Wi-Fi**

  - *Stream Fitness Videos – Platforms like YouTube or Peloton offer guided in-room workouts.*

  - *Relaxation Apps – Use Calm or Headspace to unwind after a busy day.*

- **Leverage On-Site Amenities**

  - *Hotel Gyms – Plan quick, effective workouts.*

  - *Pool Access – Swimming is a great low-impact exercise.*

  - *Local Perks – Many Airbnbs highlight nearby fitness studios or offer guest passes.*

Plane Prep: Make long flights more comfortable and productive with these tips:

- **Pack Healthy Snacks**

  - *Opt for high-protein options like nuts, protein bars, or veggies to avoid unhealthy airport food.*

- **Stay Active While You Wait**

  - *Walk the terminal or find a quiet spot for stretches or light exercises.*

- **Rest & Relaxation**

  - *Bring noise-canceling headphones and an eye mask for restful travel.*

  - *Use meditation apps or calming music to reduce stress during layovers.*

Quick Tips While Traveling (ReEmphasized)

- **Hydrate** – Drink plenty of water during long trips.

- **Stretch Regularly** – Avoid stiffness by moving during flights or car rides.

- **Prioritize Sleep** – Stick to a consistent schedule to beat travel fatigue.

- **Explore Actively** – Sightsee on foot or incorporate physical activities like hiking or biking.

Connecting Community & Keeping It Simple

Technology can save time and support your health, but its real power lies in pairing it with community and timeless habits.

Find a Virtual Community

- **Social Media:** Join fitness or wellness groups on Facebook, TikTok, or Instagram. Follow health coaches offering free live sessions or wellness tips.

- **Virtual Memberships:** Explore gyms or studios offering livestream classes.

- **Personal Trainers:** Hire a virtual trainer or join online platforms like Peloton for expert guidance. Group training with a trainer is also a great option.

Final Thought

While technology can fast-track your journey, success comes from combining smart tools with consistent habits. Tech is fused with are lives now, so work with what you got. For busy people this habit is imperative. Build your community, keep it simple, and let tech support your growth. One step, one click, and one choice at a time—you've got this!

CHAPTER 7

Time4YOU – Mastering Time Management

Feel like there just aren't enough hours in the day? Like you're stuck on a hamster wheel, running and running, but getting nowhere? Well, you're not alone. Time feels like a precious commodity, and most of us are terrible at managing it. But ALERT: You don't need more time. You just need to take control of the time you already have. Enter Time4YOU—a system I've developed to help you master time management, make space for what matters, and reclaim your life.

In this chapter, we'll explore why time management is the ultimate self-care tool and give you a sneak peek into my Time4YOU program, packed with strategies to help you take charge of your schedule. Let's make time work for YOU.

Time Management Matters

Time management isn't just about cramming more tasks into your day. It's about prioritizing what truly matters and creating space for the things that bring you joy, fulfillment, and peace. When you master your time, you:

- **Reduce Stress** – Knowing what to focus on (and what to let go of) can eliminate the overwhelm.

- **Increase Productivity** – Get more done in less time by working smarter, not harder.

- **Feel More Fulfilled** – Spend your energy on activities that align with your values and goals.

- **Create "Me Time"** – Yes, you deserve time for yourself. This isn't a luxury; it's a necessity.

Time is Money

Ineffective time management can result in missed opportunities, both professionally and personally. By managing time effectively, individuals can capitalize on opportunities that may lead to increased income or personal growth.

Let's dive into the fun, practical, and science-backed ways you can unlock your full potential with just a little more time on your side.

Value in Being Early

The early bird gets the worm, but being early gets you way more than just imaginary bird food. It means less stress, no frantic last-minute scrambles, and extra time to sip your coffee like a calm, collected, savvy boss. Mastering the art of being early isn't just about punctuality—it's a power move for better time management, sharper focus, and a whole lot more peace of mind. Another score on your health and wellness card!

More Time: Time is a finite resource, and effective time management is crucial for success. Studies indicate that individuals who manage their time well are more likely to experience higher academic performance, with a 53% higher chance of achieving better grades.

Starting your day early can provide additional time to complete important tasks, reducing the need to rush and allowing for better preparation. This approach can lead to improved health, increased happiness, and greater efficiency throughout the day.

Feeling of Accomplishment: Waking up earlier can enhance your sense of accomplishment. Completing tasks early in the day provides a sense of control and achievement, boosting self-esteem and motivation. Research suggests that individuals who effectively manage their time experience less stress and greater well-being.

Value in Being Late

There's also better late than never, and sometimes, there is a point to this. While punctuality has its perks, there's a certain value in taking your time, going with the flow, and letting life unfold at its own pace.

Better Part of the Stew is at the End: While punctuality is generally valued, there are situations where being the last to perform can be advantageous. In auditions and competitions, research indicates that participants who perform later may have a better chance of being remembered by judges. This phenomenon, known as the "recency effect," suggests that recent performances are more likely to be recalled.

Fashionably for Creatives: Being fashionably late can give you extra time to prepare, avoid unnecessary small talk, and make a grand entrance (if that's your thing). Plus, creativity doesn't always run on a strict schedule—some of the best ideas come when you're not racing against the clock.

Consequences May Motivate: Consistent tardiness can lead to negative consequences, such as missed opportunities or penalties (especially with Uncle Sam). These repercussions can serve as motivation to improve time management skills, encouraging you to start the day earlier and reduce stress.

Conquer the Ugliest Thing You Need to Do

Tackling the most challenging task first, often referred to as "eating the frog," can make the rest of the day feel more manageable. By addressing high-priority tasks early, you can build momentum and reduce procrastination. It will still linger its ugly head if you don't. Avoiding difficult tasks can lead to increased stress and anxiety. Addressing them promptly prevents them from lingering and becoming more daunting over time. Giving you time for prettier, more gorgeous things!

Urgent or Meh? Priorities

Ugh, that never-ending to-do list—some tasks scream "do me now!", while others just sit there, silently hoping you'll eventually get to them. But how do you tell the difference? Prioritizing tasks based on urgency and importance is like sorting laundry. Some things need immediate attention (that red sock in a load of whites), while others can wait (do you really need to fold those towels right now?).

The secret is understanding where to focus your energy. Urgent tasks come with tight deadlines and real consequences if ignored—paying bills, meeting work deadlines, or feeding your pet (my dog Blu definitely will remind you). Important but less urgent tasks, like finally organizing that chaotic email inbox, can be broken down and scheduled without panic.

Learning to separate the "drop everything and do it" tasks from the "this can wait" ones, you avoid unnecessary stress, boost productivity, and actually have time left over for things that matter—like binge-watching your favorite show! Ready to sort the urgent from the meh? Your sanity and streaming service provider will thank you!

Simplify, Delegate, Dominate!

Picture this (my Golden Girls moment): You're staring at that ugly to-do list. Ten things, all screaming for attention. It's overwhelming, right? So, why not do the smart thing—create a list of just one thing? Okay, it sounds too simple to work, but the magic lies in focus. When you break down your tasks into smaller, more manageable chunks, you'll not only avoid the dreaded overwhelm, but you'll also accomplish more with less stress.

But wait, there's more! Why do it all yourself when you can delegate? Not every task needs to be handled by you only and that's where the real productivity boost happens. Handing off tasks to a colleague, outsourcing, or simply asking for help, delegation frees up your time to focus on your top priority—the one thing that moves the needle. Here's why Simplify, Delegate, Dominate is important:

Less Overwhelm: Focusing on completing one task at a time can provide a sense of accomplishment and prevent feelings of being overwhelmed. This approach can lead to increased motivation and productivity.

Too Scattered, Not at Your Best: Attempting to tackle multiple tasks simultaneously can lead to decreased efficiency and quality of work. Concentrating on one task allows for better focus and performance.

Ease Up on Yourself: Recognizing the importance of self-care and not overburdening oneself with tasks is crucial for maintaining mental health and productivity.

Scheduling

Get more done the old school way of putting it on the calendar. Scheduling tasks isn't just about organizing your day; it's about making sure each task gets the time and attention it deserves. Research shows that people who block out time for their tasks are more likely to finish them efficiently, leaving procrastination in the dust. With a clear schedule, you're less likely to forget important tasks or miss deadlines, keeping those stress-induced, last-minute scramble moments to a minimum.

The real magic happens when you stick to that schedule. A well-structured calendar keeps you focused on what truly matters. Allocating specific time for each activity, ensures that your efforts align with your goals and desired outcomes. Scheduling isn't just a productivity tool—it's a secret ninja weapon for consistency, reliability, and accomplishing your goals without the overwhelm. Grab the planner or digital calendar and slay the day, one scheduled task at a time!

Apply Support Systems

Time management isn't a solo sport—it's all about building a team! It's a colleague, a friend, or an app that gently reminds you to take a break, support systems are the unsung heroes of staying on track. These little helpers keep you accountable, offer guidance, and even lighten the load when things get overwhelming (thanks to my mother and sisters for helping me with motherhood).

Educate Yourself: Continuing to learn about time management strategies and tools can enhance your skills. Resources like "Eat That Frog" by Brian Tracy offer valuable insights into effective time management.

Apply Technology: Leveraging technology can aid in time management. Here are some top-rated time management apps:

Todoist

A task management app that helps organize tasks and projects with due dates and priorities.

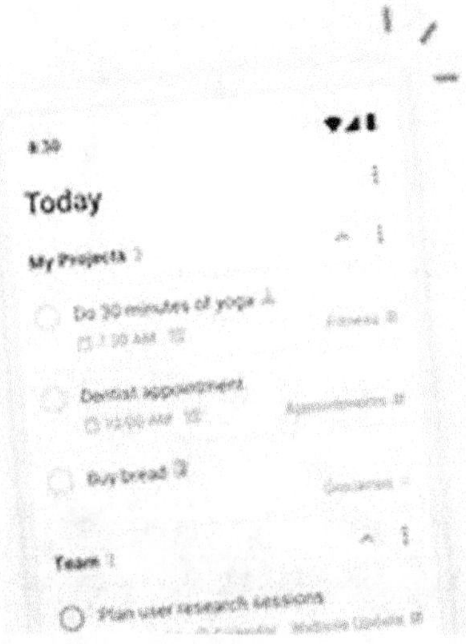

Toggl Track

A time-tracking app that allows users to monitor how much time they spend on various projects and tasks.

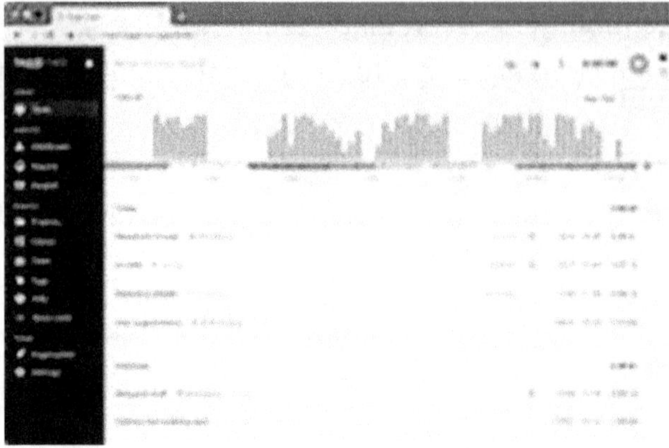

TimeTree

A shared calendar app that enables users to coordinate schedules and manage events collaboratively.

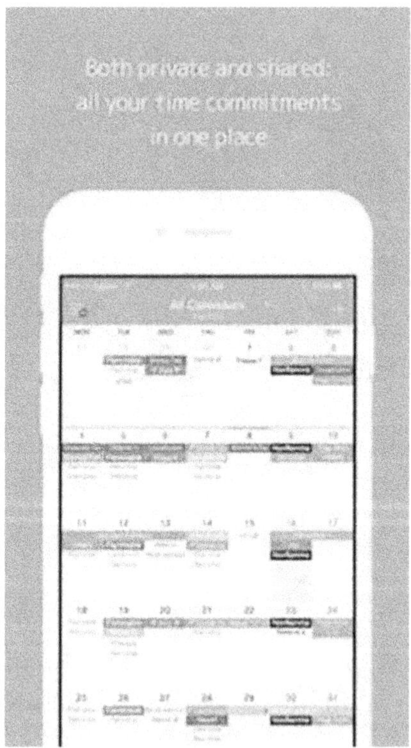

The Sneak Peek: What is Time4YOU?

Time4YOU is a practical, fun, and easy-to-follow program designed to help you take back control of your time. It's not about rigid schedules or complicated planners. Instead, it's about creating a time management system that works for YOUR unique life.

Here's a glimpse of what's inside:

1. **Your Time Inventory** – Identifying where your time is going.

2. **The Priority Pyramid** – Learning how to prioritize like a pro.

3. **The Time Blocks Technique** – Structuring your day for success.

4. **The Power of No** – Setting boundaries without guilt.

5. **Micro-Moments for Self-Care** – Finding "me time" even on the busiest days.

Let's break these down so you can start applying them today.

Step 1: Your Time Inventory

Before you can manage your time, you need to know where it's going. Think of this as auditing your schedule. Here's how to do it:

- **Track Your Time** – For one week, jot down everything you do. Be honest. Yes, this includes scrolling through Instagram or binge-watching your favorite show.

- **Categorize Tasks** – Divide your activities into categories: work, family, self-care, chores, entertainment, etc.

- **Spot Time-Wasters** – Identify areas where your time is slipping away. (Hint: Social media is the ultimate time taker!)

Fun Tip: Turn this into a game. Challenge yourself to find "bonus time" by cutting out just 30 minutes of unnecessary activities each day. That's 3.5 hours a week you can reclaim!

Step 2: The Priority Pyramid

Not all tasks are created equal. The Priority Pyramid helps you figure out what's truly important. Here's how it works:

- **Base Level: Must-Do Tasks** – These are non-negotiables, like work responsibilities or picking up the kids.

- **Middle Level: Should-Do Tasks** – These are important but can wait if needed, like organizing your closet or scheduling doctor's appointments.

- **Top Level: Want-to-Do Tasks** – These are activities that bring you joy or relaxation, like hobbies or spending time with friends.

Pro Tip: Focus on the base and middle levels first, then carve out time for the top-level activities. Don't neglect the things you love—they're what make life meaningful.

Step 3: The Time Blocks Technique

Time blocking is a simple but powerful tool to structure your day. Instead of tackling tasks randomly, you assign specific blocks of time to each activity.

How to Time Block:

- **Plan Ahead** – At the start of each day (or the night before), map out your schedule.

- **Create Focused Blocks** – Dedicate uninterrupted blocks of time to high-priority tasks. For example, "9-11 AM: Write the report."

- **Include Buffer Time** — Build in short breaks to recharge and handle unexpected interruptions.

- **Honor Your Blocks** — Treat these blocks as appointments you can't miss.

Fun Fact: Studies show that working in focused bursts (like the Pomodoro Technique) boosts productivity and prevents burnout. Try 25-minute work sessions followed by 5-minute breaks.

Step 4: The Power of No

My favorite step! One of the hardest parts of time management is learning to say "no." But here's the thing: every time you say "yes" to something, you're saying "no" to something else. Protect your time by setting boundaries.

How to Say No Gracefully:

- **Be Polite but Firm** — "I'd love to help, but I'm fully booked right now."

- **Offer an Alternative** — "I can't do this, but I can help with XYZ next week."

- **Don't Over-Explain** — A simple "no" is enough. You don't owe anyone a detailed justification.

Mindset Shift: Saying no isn't selfish. It's an act of self-care that allows you to prioritize what truly matters.

Step 5: Micro-Moments for Self-Care

Even the busiest schedules have gaps. Use these micro-moments to recharge and nurture yourself:

- **Morning Rituals** — Spend 5 minutes meditating or stretching.

- **Mindful Breaks** – Pause for a deep breath, sip tea, or enjoy a quick walk.

- **Evening Wind-Down** – Disconnect from screens and relax before bed.

Quick Idea: Set a timer for 2 minutes and focus on your breathing. You'll be amazed at how refreshed you feel.

Making Time4YOU Fun

Time management doesn't have to be boring or rigid. Here are some ways to keep it enjoyable:

- **Gamify It** – Set small challenges, like completing a task in 30 minutes or staying off your phone for an hour. Reward yourself when you succeed.

- **Use Cool Tools** – Try colorful planners, fun apps like Trello or Notion, or a quirky timer for time-blocking.

- **Celebrate Wins** – At the end of each day, reflect on what you accomplished and give yourself a pat on the back.

Final Thought

Time management isn't about perfection. It's about progress. Even small changes can make a big difference in how you feel and what you achieve. The Time4YOU program is your ticket to reclaiming your time and living a life that feels balanced, joyful, and uniquely yours. It's an honor to finally share the secrets that I actually use as a busy, working mom!

Remember, time is the one resource you can't get back. Make the most of it! Start small, stay consistent, and watch your life transform. Darling, get your groove and time back!

The Business of YOU

Welcome to the final bonus chapter of *Quick, Fast, and in a Hurry: 7 Healthy Habits for Busy People*! This chapter is all about treating yourself like the CEO of your own life. Imagine your body as your most valuable asset, and you're the business manager, visionary, and strategist, all rolled into one. Just like running a successful business requires a solid plan, core habits, and follow-through, your life needs the same attention—without the corporate jargon. It's time to manage your health, happiness, and goals like a pro, or how about, like a boss!

1. Treat Yourself Like You Would Your Own Business or Profession

Just as a business owner prioritizes success, you need to prioritize your own health and well-being. If you wouldn't skip an important meeting with a major client, why should you neglect your own needs? Treat your daily habits and decisions like a personal business strategy. Schedule time for self-care, create healthy routines, and invest in yourself like you would any valuable asset. After all, a thriving business depends on its most valuable resource—YOU!

2. The Economics of You: Generate Healthy Revenue

True wealth isn't just about money—it's about the health, joy, relationships, and energy you generate every day. Think of your body as a bank, and every healthy choice you make—whether it's eating well, exercising, or resting—is an investment that pays dividends. When you nurture yourself, you have the vitality to accomplish everything you need and more, just like a profitable business.

3. Mission Statement, Strategies, and Team/Departments

A business without a mission statement is just a collection of tasks. Similarly, a life without purpose can feel directionless. Create your own personal mission statement—what do you want to accomplish, and how will your health play a role? Break down your goals into strategies and build your "team"—a support system of friends, mentors, and professionals who keep you accountable. No successful business runs solo, and neither should you!

4. Choose Health First

Without health, nothing else matters. Prioritize habits that nourish your mind, body, and spirit. From personal experience, I can tell you that nothing is more important than your well-being. A healthy you is the key to achieving all your goals. Small, consistent habits lead to big changes. Health is wealth—so don't skimp on it.

5. Review Your Progress and Hiccups

Running a business means checking in on your progress and identifying areas that need improvement. Do the same for your health journey. Reflect on your successes and setbacks. Track your habits, write them down, and look back on how far you've come. Every hiccup is an opportunity to refine and adjust. Consistency is key—even when progress feels slow, you're still moving forward.

6. Be Kind to Yourself

Treat yourself with the same kindness and respect that you would give a close friend. You are your own biggest cheerleader. When you slip up, give yourself grace, and when you win, celebrate your victories. You define your worth, not anyone else. You're a unique miracle with talents that no one else has—honor that and don't let life's demands strip you of your self-worth.

7. Stay in the Present

While learning from the past and planning for the future is important, don't lose yourself in them. Happiness, fulfillment, and creativity all beat in the present moment. Stop dwelling on past mistakes or overthinking the future. Focus on today—on what you can do, feel, and be right now. Let the future excite you, but don't let it overshadow the potential of the present.

8. It's NEVER Too Late for New Ventures or Dreams

Age or adversity? Forget those limiting beliefs! It's never too late to start something new or chase a fresh dream. Society's timelines or your own doubts shouldn't hold you back. Stay curious, dream big, and embrace new opportunities. The world is full of them—no matter your age or circumstances. I'm living proof that it's never too late to turn your dreams into reality.

9. What Are Your Surroundings and What Are You Feeding Yourself?

You are what you consume—mentally, emotionally, and physically. Turn off the noise—be it toxic social media feeds, news cycles, or energy-draining people. Instead, surround yourself with uplifting content, inspiring books, and positive people. What you allow into your space directly impacts your mindset and health, so be intentional about it.

10. Laugh and Use Humor

Laughter is one of the best stress-busters. It lowers stress, boosts mood, and opens you up to new perspectives. Life can feel overwhelming, but finding humor in everyday moments helps keep things in perspective. Use humor to navigate tough situations—it makes challenges seem more manageable and, most importantly, it feels great!

11. Make Stress Management a Priority

Stress is the silent killer of health, productivity, and relationships. Make stress management a daily habit—whether through deep breathing, yoga, journaling, or mindfulness. The less stress controls you, the more you'll enjoy your health, work, and relationships.

12. Keep in Mind That We Are All Connected

We're all part of the same universal energy. We share dreams, struggles, and aspirations. Understanding this helps you feel less isolated and more connected to others. Whether reaching out for support or collaborating with others, remember—we're all in this together. Find strength in community and support each other along the journey.

Final Thought

You've read the tips and hacks, but here's the truth—you're still busy. Deadlines, meetings, to-do lists—yep, they're still there. And that's okay! You don't have to be perfect. The key is to make time for yourself amid the busyness. Treat your health like a top priority, take action, and give yourself grace. After all, you're the CEO of your life, and no successful CEO forgets to take care of their most valuable asset—YOU.

Your Busy Life, Transformed

Well, look at you! You've made it to the finish line of *Quick, Fast, and in a Hurry: 7 Healthy Habits for Busy People*, and I hope you're feeling a little more empowered, energized, and ready to take on life's madness with a whole new outlook. But before you rush off to conquer your to-do list, let's pause for a moment. This isn't the end—it's the beginning of a new chapter in your life, one where you're the star of your own show, managing your health, happiness, and hustle like a pro.

I know life can feel like a never-ending sprint, and you probably don't have time for an additional hour at the gym or to meal-prep for the week. But here's the magic: small, intentional habits are your secret weapon. They may seem tiny at first, but trust me—they add up in a big way. These habits aren't meant to make you perfect, because let's be honest, who wants to be perfect anyway? Perfection is overrated. Instead, these habits are about progress. And you're already making progress just by picking up this book and committing to yourself. Seriously, that's huge!

Let's Break It Down: Your 7 Healthy Habits

Habit 1: Fuel Up the Mind – This habit is your foundation. You've learned how to reignite your inner spark, staying motivated even when life throws its curveballs. Whether you're balancing career, family, or side hustles, you're ready to face challenges with clarity and purpose.

Habit 2: Move Your Body – Your body is not a machine; it's a powerhouse. No matter how busy you get, you deserve to move, stretch, and energize yourself. Small movements can have a big impact on your well-being, and you've learned that keeping your body active doesn't require a full workout every day—just consistency.

Habit 3: Watch Your Mouth – Making healthy food choices doesn't have to be complicated. You don't need to become a full-time chef; instead, you've discovered how to fuel your body with healthy foods that nourish you without feeling overwhelmed.

Habit 4: Check Your Surroundings – This habit reminds you that your environment plays a crucial role in your well-being. The people you surround yourself with—your family, friends, colleagues—shape your experiences. By creating a supportive and nurturing environment, you elevate your mental, emotional, and physical health.

Habit 5: Press Pause – Life is fast-paced, but slowing down is essential. Taking time to recharge isn't lazy; it's necessary. Habit 5 gives you permission to hit pause, reset, and recover so you can return to life's demands with more energy and focus.

Habit 6: Work With What You Got – Technology can either drain your time or enhance your life. With Habit 6, you've learned how to use technology as a tool that works for you—helping you track meals, set reminders, and stay organized, so you have more time and mental space for what matters.

Habit 7: Time4YOU – No matter how busy you are, carving out time for yourself is non-negotiable. Time is your most valuable resource, and you now have the tools to prioritize self-care, ensuring you don't burn out while managing everything else on your plate.

BONUS Habit: The Business of You

This bonus habit is a game-changer. It's about approaching your life with the mindset of a CEO—taking charge of your well-being, your time, and your priorities. You are the leader of your own life, and when you treat yourself as such, you unlock the potential to achieve amazing things. You are not just managing your schedule; you're actively building a life that aligns with your core values, goals, and health.

What's Next?

Here's the thing: Life will never slow down. There will always be more emails, more meetings, more responsibilities, more everything. But now, you have the tools to handle it with grace and energy. It's not about adding more to your plate, it's about mastering the art of balancing what matters most.

So what's next? Keep these habits close, use them when you need a little boost, and don't be afraid to adjust as life shifts. You've got the blueprint now, and trust me, you're not just surviving— you're thriving. And here's a little secret: It's all about having fun with it! Life doesn't have to be a grind. With the healthy habits from Quick, Fast, and in a Hurry, you'll create a life that feels lighter, brighter, and way more fulfilling. You deserve to have it all: success, joy, energy, and most importantly, health.

So go ahead—make today the day you start living this journey, not just rushing through it. You're ready. You've got this, and the world is waiting for you to show up as your best, healthiest, and most balanced self. **LET'S GO!**

JASMIN HAYNES, MBA
Author l Speaker l Coach